TOTAL YOUTH MINISTRY

MINISTRY RESOURCES FOR

Pastoral Care

Pray It! Study It! Live It!™ resources offer a holistic approach
to learning, living, and passing on the Catholic faith.

The Total Faith™ Initiative

Total Catechesis
Catechetical Sessions on Christian Morality
Catechetical Sessions on Christian Prayer
Catechetical Sessions on Liturgy and the Sacraments
Catechetical Sessions on the Creed

Total Youth Ministry
Ministry Resources for Community Life
Ministry Resources for Evangelization
Ministry Resources for Justice and Service
Ministry Resources for Pastoral Care
Ministry Resources for Prayer and Worship
Ministry Resources for Youth Leadership Development

Total Faith™ Initiative Coordinator's Manual

The Catholic Faith Handbook for Youth

The Catholic Youth Bible™

TOTAL YOUTH MINISTRY

MINISTRY RESOURCES FOR

Pastoral Care

Marilyn Kielbasa

saint mary's press

The publishing team included Laurie Delgatto, development editor; Barbara Murray, contributing editor; Laurie Berg-Shaner, copy editor; Barbara Bartelson, production editor; Cären Yang, art director and designer; Jonathan Thomas Goebel, cover designer; Digital Images © PhotoDisc, Inc., cover images; Alan S. Hanson, prepress specialist; Elly Poppe, CD-ROM developer; manufacturing coordinated by the production services department of Saint Mary's Press.

Produced with the assistance of settingPace, LLC, Cincinnati, Ohio.

Ministry resource manuals were developed in collaboration with the Center for Ministry Development. The publishing team included Thomas East, project coordinator.

Printed in the United States of America

2463

ISBN 978-0-88489-770-5

Contents

Part C: Strategies for Effective Pastoral Care of Youth

Introduction

About Total Youth Ministry

Many youth today are waiting to hear the Good News that is ours as Christ's disciples. Youth in our parishes long to grow spiritually and to belong to their family, Church, and local community in meaningful ways. Parents of youth long to experience Church as supportive of and caring about the same things they care about. They hope the parish will offer ways for youth to be involved and to grow in their faith. Parents want to understand youth ministry so they can support and encourage their child's participation.

Parishes want to know how to include youth and how to pass on faith to a new generation. Parish members want to see youth more involved, and are worried about the challenges that face today's youth. They know that young people need support from their faith community—now more than ever. Parish youth ministry leaders are generous, passionate, and busy people; they make sacrifices so that youth will have a community to belong to and a place to grow. They need ideas and plans for youth ministry activities—and strategies that really work. They are working toward a ministry that goes beyond just gathering groups of young people; they are working toward a ministry that makes connections between youth and the community.

All those voices have something in common—a longing for youth ministry that is inclusive, dynamic, and flexible.

In 1997 the United States Conference of Catholic Bishops (USCCB) published its blueprint for youth ministry in the twenty-first century. *Renewing the Vision: A Framework for Catholic Youth Ministry* challenges youth ministry to focus its efforts in these directions:

- to empower young people to live as disciples of Jesus Christ in our world today
- to draw young people to responsible participation in the life, mission, and work of the Catholic faith community
- to foster the total personal and spiritual growth of each young person

In *Renewing the Vision*, the bishops urge the Church to guide young people toward a life of fullness in Jesus Christ, and to give them the tools that will enable them to live out that fullness as Catholic Christians. To put it simply, the bishops call young people to embrace their faith as they study it, pray it, and live it. The bishops also challenge the faith community to surround young people with love, care, and attention and to include youth throughout the life of the parish.

The Ministry Resource Manuals

The ministry resource manuals of the Total Youth Ministry series address each of the components of youth ministry as outlined in *Renewing the Vision*. The advocacy and catechesis components are woven throughout the ministry resource manuals. You will find the following information in each of the ministry resource manuals:

- a chapter explaining the component, connecting it to Church documents, and identifying practical ideas and resources for implementing the component
- sessions that can stand alone or be combined with others in the series
- numerous strategies, ideas, suggestions, and resources that go beyond a specific gathering

The content of each manual includes newly developed sessions, ideas and strategies as well as "tried and true" material drawn or adapted from *Youth-Works* and other resources previously published by the Center for Ministry Development.

Following is a brief description of each of the manuals:

- *Ministry Resources for Community Life* offers faith communities program resources and strategies to build community among young people and throughout the entire parish. The resource includes nine gathered sessions to help young people get to know one another, themselves, and the meaning of Christian community. It also contains an outline for an ecumenical event to help build community across denominational lines, and it offers practical strategies and ideas to help manage community issues, make the most of community life opportunities, and encourage intergenerational and family relationships.
- *Ministry Resources for Evangelization* offers faith communities tools and program resources to evangelize youth. It offers practical strategies and ideas for outreach to young people and contains twelve gathered sessions to share the Good News. It also includes a retreat to engage young people in becoming or continuing as Jesus' disciples.
- *Ministry Resources for Justice and Service* offers faith communities programs and strategies to engage youth in justice, direct service, and advocacy in faithful, age-appropriate, and proactive ways. This resource contains eight gathered sessions around specific justice issues, an overnight retreat

on service to poor people, and two half-day retreats or evening reflections on simplicity and racism.

- At the heart of *Ministry Resources for Pastoral Care* are twelve sessions designed to equip young people with the tools needed to celebrate their holy goodness and navigate some of life's difficult issues. The topics of the sessions include recognizing the goodness in oneself and others, building and maintaining relationships, dealing with tough times, and preparing for the future. The last section of the manual comprises strategies for doing the ongoing work of pastoral care.

- *Ministry Resources for Prayer and Worship* is designed for those who work with and walk with youth in this journey of discipleship. The manual contains three sessions to teach youth to pray and to practice praying in different forms. Eleven communal prayer services are included, which can be used on a variety of occasions throughout the seasons of the year. The manual also contains strategies and resources to help youth communities develop patterns of prayer and to include youth in preparing prayers and liturgies.

- *Ministry Resources for Youth Leadership Development* offers faith communities program resources and strategies to develop youth as leaders within youth ministry programs and the parish. The manual includes four foundational sessions on Christian leadership, ten leadership skill sessions and minisessions, and two sessions to help prepare youth and adults for working together. The manual offers ideas and strategies for creating leadership roles within the parish, inviting youth to leadership, and working with the parents of youth leaders. The plans for implementing sessions and other gathered events are complete, easy to follow, and adaptable to your community.

With the detailed plans provided for the sessions, activities, and strategies in Total Youth Ministry, youth ministry volunteers no longer need to be program designers. By using the Total Youth Ministry resources, you can focus on the important task of finding the leaders who make youth ministry happen. Each session includes an overview, a list of materials, preparation steps, and step-by-step instructions for facilitating a session with confidence. Most sessions also include a variety of ways to extend the theme of the session with prayer, related learning exercises, or follow-through experiences.

An Added Feature: CD-ROMs

Each manual has a CD-ROM that includes the full content of the manual and is in read-only, non-print format. Handouts are provided in printable color versions (which cannot be customized) and in black-and-white versions that you can customize for the particular needs of a group. You will also find hyperlinks to suggested Web sites.

Participant Resources

Much of the material in the ministry resource manuals is designed to work in a complementary way with the contents of *The Catholic Faith Handbook for Youth (CFH)* and *The Catholic Youth Bible (CYB)*.

Ministry Resources for Pastoral Care: An Overview

Effective pastoral care has three dimensions. The first is promotion and prevention, which includes training in life skills and being proactive in promoting healthy adolescent development. The second is caring for youth who are in crisis and providing direct assistance to youth who are in need. The third is advocacy, or developing strategies for challenging systems.

The focus of this manual is primarily on the first task, promotion and prevention. The twelve sessions in part B of this manual are designed to foster life skills in young people, giving youth the tools to build and maintain relationships and to deal with some of life's challenges.

Part C of this manual addresses the other two tasks of pastoral care. It includes a variety of strategies for connecting young people with the communities in which they live, providing resources for families with teens, and advocating for the inclusion of young people in all dimensions of the Church.

Manual Contents

Part A: Pastoral Care: An Overview

Chapter 1: Pastoral Care and Youth Ministry

This essay describes a broad understanding of the pastoral care component of youth ministry, including the five key principles and three interdependent elements that guide the development of pastoral care with adolescents.

Part B: Pastoral Care Sessions

This section includes twelve sessions for developing life skills and positive attitudes in young people.

Study It

The core sessions in this manual are 60 minutes long. The sessions are not sequential, so you may organize them in a way that is most appropriate for your situation.

Each session begins with a brief overview, a list of expected outcomes, and a list of recommended background reading, followed by a checklist of the preparation required, including all materials needed. A complete description of the session procedure is then provided, including all activities and discussions, prayer, and some Live It options.

Within each session you may find additional resources, including options for extending the session through supplemental activities. Music resources are available from a variety of publishers, and a Bible concordance will provide additional citations if you want to add a more substantial scriptural component to a session. *The Saint Mary's Press Essential Bible Concordance* offers a simple, user-friendly index to key words in the Bible. Many of the sessions provide a list of media resources—such as print, video, and Internet—for more exploration. Family approaches provide simple follow-up suggestions for family learning, enrichment, celebration, prayer, and service.

Pray It

Each session also offers opportunities and suggestions for prayer that is focused on the session's theme, as well as lists of musical selections from *Spirit & Song.* Prayer forms include guided meditation, shared prayer, music, silence, prayer by young people, reflective reading, and experiences created by the participants. The Pray It component gives the young people an opportunity to bring their insights and concerns to God in prayer. The time frame for prayer experiences varies from 15 to 20 minutes.

Live It

This manual can be a springboard for connections with other youth ministry experiences. Therefore all the sessions include additional strategies to support the learning process. Those activities can be used to extend the session, provide good follow-up for the Study It core activities, and allow for age-appropriate assimilation of the material.

Session Overviews

Chapter 2: Faith and Friendship
- This session considers the basic qualities of friendship and invites the participants to consider the differences between acquaintances, friends, and intimate, or close, friends.

Chapter 3: Made in God's Image
- This session invites the young people to name the ways they make a difference in the world as children of God and parts of God's plan for the universe. It also encourages them to analyze the negative messages they get from the media and our culture.

Chapter 4: Dating Relationships
- The point of this session is to get the teens thinking about the topic of dating relationships in purposeful ways, so that they might avoid some of the pitfalls of relationships that move too fast or get stuck at a certain

level, in which partners have different expectations, or that are hurtful. Throughout the session the young people are urged to think about what is emotionally appropriate and what will bring growth to the dating relationship and to the individuals who are involved in it.

Chapter 5: Accepting and Honoring Others

- The point of this session is to raise awareness of emotional needs and the harm that is caused when people do not honor those needs in themselves and others.

Chapter 6: Choices and Decisions

- This session provides a decision-making process that, if followed carefully, can help teens make choices that will lead to a holy, happy, and healthy life.

Chapter 7: Managing Life's Ups and Downs

- This session provides the participants with the tools to understand and deal with the stresses they face, that is, the changes, challenges, and occasional crises that are part of everyone's lives.

Chapter 8: Handling Anger, Managing Conflict

- This session gives the young people the opportunity to explore their attitudes toward anger and to learn a process for evaluating and addressing conflicts in a positive and appropriate way.

Chapter 9: Dealing with Life's Changes

- This session helps the teens identify and deal with positive and negative changes and the resulting losses, and teaches them valuable coping skills.

Chapter 10: Parent-Teen Communication: An Intergenerational Session

- This intergenerational session invites parents and teenagers to seek out and develop effective communication skills for peaceful living and healthy growth.

Chapter 11: Helping Peers in Crisis

- This session builds on teens' natural tendency toward relationship, and gives them some tools to help friends who are struggling.

Chapter 12: Sexuality and Spirituality

- The purpose of this session is to help the participants understand the concept of sexual integrity as the ideal way to achieve the fullness of life of which Jesus speaks. They will also think about setting boundaries in their relationships that will help them achieve that goal.

Chapter 13: Finding Hope

- This session is about helping the young people see the connections between happiness, hope, and faith, and the role those elements play in bringing them closer to eternal life. It also helps them recognize internal and external sources of hope that they can draw on when needed.

Part C: Strategies for Effective Pastoral Care of Youth

Chapter 14: Pastoral Care of Youth

This chapter offers twelve suggestions for promoting positive youth development that go beyond the life-skills training offered in the sessions. Some of the topics are helping parents and families, networking within the community, promoting positive values, and participating in the life of the faith community.

Chapter 15: Retreats and Extended Events

This chapter combines sessions from part B into extended formats, including two daylong retreats and one extended session. In addition, it offers five more options for combining sessions.

Chapter 16: Supporting Young People and Families in Crisis

This chapter offers principles for providing care to young people who are in crisis, as well as a variety of ideas and strategies that provide resources and support for families that are facing alcoholism, drug addiction, eating disorders, sexual abuse, depression, suicide, and divorce.

Handouts and Resources

All the necessary handouts and resources for a chapter are found at the end of that chapter in the manual. They are also found on the accompanying CD-ROM, in both color and black-and-white versions. The black-and-white materials may be customized to suit your particular needs.

Facilitating the Sessions

Inviting Youth

The most effective invitation is a personal one—inviting a young person to the session directly, by phone, e-mail, or direct personal contact. The best invitations come from young people who invite their friends and others to join them at the session.

Hospitality

Hospitality needs to be a part of every aspect of the gathering: in the invitations and promotional materials (by using inclusive language and images), in the welcoming of participants to the session, and in the relationships between youth and adults. If the young people do not know one another well, include warm-up activities to help them get to know one another in a nonthreatening way.

It is also essential to create a hospitable learning environment so that the young people feel comfortable disclosing their thoughts. In a session on an issue related to pastoral care, the more comfortable and welcome a young person feels, the more likely she or he will be to go beyond the surface when sharing personal experiences.

Preparing Yourself

Read each session or activity before you facilitate it; then use it creatively to meet the needs of the young people in your group. Knowing your audience will help you determine which activities will work best for it. Some of the activities require preparation; allow yourself adequate time to get ready.

All the sessions include presentations of key concepts and teachings. The session plans offer guidelines for these talks. Preparing for the presentations is vital to the success of each session. Ensure that the presentations are effective by practicing them ahead of time. Familiarize yourself with the material and invite constructive criticism from other leaders. Personalize the materials by adding your own stories and examples.

Standard Materials

To save time, consider gathering frequently used materials in bins and storing those bins in a place that is accessible to all staff and volunteer leaders. Here are some recommendations for organizing the bins.

Supply Bin

The following items appear frequently in the materials checklists:
- *The Catholic Youth Bible,* at least one copy for every two participants
- *The Catholic Faith Handbook for Youth,* one copy for your reference
- masking tape
- cellophane tape
- washable and permanent markers (thick-line and thin-line)
- pens or pencils
- self-stick notes
- scissors
- newsprint
- blank paper, scrap paper, and notebook paper
- journals, one for each participant
- index cards
- baskets
- candles and matches
- items to create a prayer space (for example, a colored cloth, a cross, a bowl for water, and a vase for flowers)

Music Bin

Young people often find profound meaning in the music and lyrics of songs, both past and present. Also, the right music can set the appropriate mood for a prayer or an activity. Begin with a small collection of tapes or

CDs in a music bin, and add to it over time. You might ask the young people to put some of their favorite music in the bin. The bin might include the following styles of music:

- *Prayerful, reflective instrumental music,* such as the kind that is available in the adult alternative section of music stores. Labels that specialize in this type of music include Windham Hill and Narada.
- *Popular songs with powerful messages.* If you are not well versed in popular music, ask the young people to offer suggestions.
- *The music of contemporary Catholic artists.* Many teens are familiar with the work of Catholic musicians such as Steve Angrisano, Sarah Hart, David W. Kauffman, Michael Mahler, Jesse Manibusan, and Danielle Rose.

Also consider including songbooks and hymnals. Many of the musical selections suggested in Total Youth Ministry are taken from the *Spirit & Song* hymnal, published by Oregon Catholic Press (OCP). If you wish to order copies of this hymnal, please contact OCP directly at *www.ocp.org* or by calling 800-548-8749. Including copies of your parish's chosen hymnal is a suitable option as well. You might also check with your liturgy or music director for recordings of parish hymns.

Some Closing Thoughts

We hope you find this material helpful as you help young people deal with the immense challenges they face, as well as celebrate with them their holy goodness and the constant presence of God in their lives. Please be assured of our continual prayers for you and the young people you serve.

Your Comments or Suggestions

Saint Mary's Press wants to know your reactions to the materials in the Total Youth Ministry series. We are open to all kinds of suggestions, including these:

- an alternative way to conduct an activity
- an audiovisual or other media resource that worked well with this material
- a book or an article you found helpful
- an original activity or process
- a prayer experience or service
- a helpful preparation for other leaders
- an observation about the themes or content of this material

If you have a comment or suggestion, please write to us at 702 Terrace Heights, Winona, MN 55987-1318; call us at our toll-free number, 800-533-8095; or e-mail us at *smp@smp.org*. Your ideas will help improve future editions of Total Youth Ministry.

Part A

Pastoral Care: An Overview

Pastoral Care and Youth Ministry

Pastoral care has long been a part of the foundation of parish ministry, including its ministry to young people. It is a process of attending to the needs of teenagers, their families, and the parish community. The scriptural foundation of pastoral care is the Emmaus story from Luke's Gospel (24:13–25). Pastoral care involves healing, reconciling, sustaining, confronting, guiding, and informing.

The following five key principles guide the development of pastoral care with adolescents.

Pastoral Care Is Not Counseling

All adults who work with youth must be pastoral caregivers, that is, they should be capable of integrating sound theological principles with good interpersonal skills and programming. This requires strong self-knowledge, an understanding of the adolescent experience and family systems, and a caring stance toward young people.

Another important skill for pastoral caregivers is knowing when the services of a trained mental-health professional are needed. When a young person's difficulties are beyond the realm of pastoral care, the caregiver has a responsibility to connect the person with someone who is trained in the skills of intervention, diagnosis, and counseling.

Pastoral Care Goes Beyond Crises

Pastoral care is part of an ongoing relationship. It is proactive rather than reactive. Those of us in youth ministry are continually challenged to look for new opportunities to care for teens and give them the necessary tools for living a holy, happy, and healthy life. Situational crisis points may arise that demand a certain expertise, but an ongoing pastoral presence is also required.

We must be intentional about integrating pastoral care approaches and programs into a comprehensive youth ministry. We must reexamine the quality of our presence to and with young people, and make needed changes. Pastoral care is a stance, a lens, and a starting point for ministry.

Pastoral Care Is Everyone's Responsibility

Pastoral care moves beyond parish and school boundaries to include local, diocesan, and even national attention. Many young people are at risk because they live in poverty, see and experience violence, lack support systems, and have limited positive choices. Pastoral care of youth must be a collaborative effort between the parish and the community. We all need to own the vision of caring for the holistic needs of youth. We must be welcoming, hospitable, caring communities. Community networks must be established and resources shared.

Pastoral Care Must Help Youth Develop Life Skills

Developing life skills in adolescents is an essential element of youth formation in families and in communities. However, we can become compartmentalized in our thinking about which youth-serving agencies are responsible for which aspects of youth development. Consequently many adolescents are never taught skills that will help them cope and plan. We must work together to identify and develop in youth the intrapersonal, interpersonal, and systemic skills that are essential to their survival and success.

Pastoral Care Must Address the Needs of Families

Family structures and systems have changed tremendously in the last fifty years. Parents are often not equipped to deal with their own identity issues, much less with their children's. Family structures are frequently shuffled at the same time that teenagers are trying to identify where they belong in the larger scheme.

Parents and teenagers need time and space, a caring environment, and caring professionals with whom to explore those issues. Families may also benefit from things like support groups, education about adolescent development, family activities, or latchkey programs for younger teens. Family ministry and youth ministry need to join forces to deal with the complex issues associated with raising teenagers in the twenty-first century.

Those five principles describe a broad understanding of the component of youth ministry known as pastoral care. To achieve that comprehensive vision, we must include three interdependent elements in our parish and school programs:

- *Promotion and prevention.* Offer training in life skills and proactively promote healthy adolescent development.
- *Care for youth in crisis.* Have resources available to respond to youth who are in crisis and to provide direct assistance to youth who are in need.
- *Advocacy.* Developing strategies for challenging systems.

A pastoral care approach calls for an ongoing process of caring deeply and confronting honestly, of meeting people where they are and showing them the rich possibilities of human wholeness. It is the call for adolescents to believe in themselves because someone else already believes in them. Jesus related to people in terms of what they could become as well as who they already were. His ability to see and affirm the potential within each person helped people find the courage to become caring followers and dynamic leaders. Certainly with that same attention, young people are capable of doing the same!

Part B

Pastoral Care Sessions

2 Faith and Friendship

AT A GLANCE

Study It

**Core Session:
Acquaintances, Friends,
and Intimate Friends**
(60 minutes)

Pray It

◆ Relationship Builders
and Blockers
(15 minutes)

Live It

◆ Scripture search
◆ Creative friendship
◆ Love and friendship
◆ Trust exercise
◆ Helpful friends
◆ Jesus' relationships
◆ Friendship through
the years
◆ Life-giving relationships

Overview

Friendship plays a dynamic role in the life of an adolescent. Yet some young people feel that their friendships are incomplete. Others feel pulled in too many directions by their friends. And some are still unsure about what makes for good friendship. This session considers the basic qualities of friendship and invites the participants to consider the differences between acquaintances, friends, and intimate, or close, friends. It encourages the young people to discuss characteristics of those relationships and explore ways to develop and nurture them.

Outcomes

◆ The participants will articulate the difference between acquaintances, friends, and intimate friends.
◆ The participants will identify relationships in their lives that require additional time and energy.

Background Reading

◆ Scriptural connections: Sir. 6:5–17 (friendship, false and true), John 17:6–26 (Jesus prays for his friends.), Phil. 1:3–11 (Paul's greeting to his friends in Philippi), Col. 3:12–17 (friendship in Christ)
◆ *Catholic Youth Bible* article connections: "Friends, Old and New" (Sir. 9:10), "Faithful Friends" (Mark 2:1–12), "A Prayer for Friends" (John, chap. 17), "Friendship" (Phil. 1:3–11)

Study it!

Core Session: Acquaintances, Friends, and Intimate Friends (60 minutes)

Try This

As part of the session opener, include a music collage of parts of popular songs that deal with friendship. You might begin with bits of oldies songs and end with present-day hits.

Preparation
- Gather the following items:
  - ❑ blank paper
  - ❑ pens or pencils
  - ❑ newsprint
  - ❑ markers
  - ❑ masking tape
  - ❑ copies of handout 1, "Circles of Relationships," one for each participant
  - ❑ a *Catholic Youth Bible* or other Bible
- Make a continuum on newsprint, with the words "Acquaintance" and "Intimate Friend" at opposite ends.

1. Give each young person a blank sheet of paper and a pen or pencil. Explain that the theme of the session is friendship. Ask the participants to think about a few people whom they consider to be friends and what it is about those people that makes them good friends. After a short reflection time, tell them to write five qualities that they think are important in a friend. They should do this silently and on their own.

2. Divide the teens into small groups. Give each group a sheet of newsprint and markers. Explain that each group has the task of developing a list of the characteristics of a good friend. It should begin by having everyone share their lists of five qualities. Then the group is to discuss all the qualities on the lists of the group members, and come up with one list of the five most important qualities in a friend. Those five qualities should be written on newsprint. Allow about 10 minutes for this part of the activity.

3. Invite each group to post its newsprint list. Allow time for the participants to look over the lists, and then lead a discussion of the following questions:
- Do the qualities of friendship listed on newsprint apply to all relationships in life?
- If not, what makes other relationships different from friendship?

4. Post the continuum that you created before the session. Summarize the following information in your own words. Include the participants' thoughts from the previous step.

- What many people call friendship is actually a part of a continuum of relationships, starting with acquaintance, moving through friendship and greater degrees of self-disclosure and closeness to intimacy.
- Many people relate the term *intimacy* to sexual or romantic relationships. But it is more properly used to designate a deep, close relationship with someone of either gender.
- The word *acquaintance* designates a person we know casually. We do not know much about him or her, and we haven't revealed much of ourselves to him or her.
- Although it is easy to define the differences between acquaintanceship and friendship, it is often more difficult to define the differences between friendship and intimacy.
- Friendship is a relationship characterized by the following qualities:
  - firm loyalty
  - mutual trust
  - shared vision, experience, or history
- Intimacy—or close friendship—builds on friendship. Thus, the first three characteristics are the same. What makes a relationship intimate or close are these two additional qualities:
  - a deep and mutual self-disclosure, that is, a willingness on the part of both friends to share deep feelings, thoughts, hopes, or fears
  - a shared vulnerability, or acceptance of the risks that sharing the deepest part of oneself can bring
- When two people in a relationship do not share the same level of self-disclosure or vulnerability, the relationship is often scarred or dysfunctional.
- All relationships do not have intimacy as their goal. Only a few friendships will move to intimate status. Close friendships may even move from intimacy back to simple friendship after a while, particularly as friends move on to other interests or move apart.
- The continuum also extends beyond the ends defined here. Beyond our acquaintances is the world of strangers, that is, the whole human race. Our attitude toward this group is a measure of our character. How we treat people we do not know, no matter where they live, reflects our understanding of and commitment to God's message.
- At the other end is one of the deepest forms of intimacy: solitude, or intimacy with self. Many would say that people cannot sustain an intimate friendship without the ability to be intimate with themselves. Also, solitude is the place where one develops an intimacy with God.

VARIATION:
Gender Groups

- ◆ Divide the large group by gender, and give each gender group a sheet of newsprint and markers. Tell the girls that they are to write a list of the characteristics of friendship between males. Direct the boys to list the characteristics of friendship between females. Discuss the results, and give each gender a chance to ask questions and offer clarifications. Follow with a discussion of the benefits and challenges of boy-girl friendships.
- ◆ Have each gender group find pictures or ads in magazines that typify friendships between people of its gender. Discuss the differences between masculine and feminine approaches to friendship.

- Our relationship with God is reflected in all our relationships. Our belief that all people are made in the image and likeness of God demands that we treat others respectfully and honor their place in the universe. Our ability to be intimate with God allows us to be in deep relationship with others. It also calls us to a place of solitude where we can be at one with God.

5. Distribute handout 1, "Circles of Relationships." Review the directions with the young people, and invite them to move to a place in the room where they can be alone with their thoughts as they complete the handout.

6. Ask the participants to return to their small groups and discuss the results of the handout. Encourage them to focus the discussion on the areas they need to work on rather than on specific people or relationships. For example, they might talk about how to develop a deeper level of trust with a friend, how to increase the number of people with whom they have a casual acquaintance relationship, or how to increase the level of self-disclosure with someone they consider to be a close friend.

7. Gather the young people in one group, and invite volunteers to name some of the things they would like to develop in their friendships. Then invite the participants to share responses to the following sentence starters:

- I learned that . . .
- I discovered that . . .
- I still have questions about . . .
- I feel confident about developing friendships in my life because . . .
- I feel hesitant about developing friendships in my life because . . .
- I will use what I have learned in the coming week by . . .

8. Conclude the session by reading Sir. 6:14–16. If you have a copy of *The Catholic Youth Bible,* also read the article "Friends," located near the passage.

Try This

Instead of completing the sentence starters in step 7 in the large group, try one of the following options, each of which will give everyone an opportunity to voice their thoughts:

- Assign a partner to each teen, and have the pairs discuss their answers with each other.
- Do the exercise as a journal activity.
- Distribute index cards. Have the young people write each sentence starter and its answer on a separate card. Collect the cards, organize them by sentence starter, and recruit several teens to read the answers. Discuss the results.

Spirit & Song connections

- "Lean on Me," by Bill Withers
- "We Gotta Love," by Tom Booth, Israel Houghton, and Matt Maher

Pray It

Relationship Builders and Blockers (15 minutes)

You will need ample space for this prayer experience, so that the participants can gather in a circle and then move back from that circle.

Preparation

- Create a prayer space with a Bible, a lighted candle, and a cross or an icon of Jesus. You may also want to add some symbols of friendship, such as a yearbook, a telephone, or photos.
- Recruit a volunteer to read Sir. 6:5–17.
- Choose a song about friendship to play at the end of the prayer. Ask the young people for suggestions.

1. Gather the young people in a circle around the prayer space. Ask them to put their arms around one another's shoulders. Invite the person you recruited before the session to read the passage from Sirach.

2. Tell the young people that you are going to lead them through a reflection on the relationships in their life. Ask them to think about all the people whose names they wrote in the concentric circles on handout 1 during the core session. After a few minutes, explain that you will read several statements. They are to respond honestly, as directed. Encourage them to maintain a quiet prayerfulness. Then read the following statements, pausing for a moment after each one:

- Healthy friendships are necessary for all of us. Through the people in our lives, we can experience comfort, fun, learning, laughter, challenges, growth, and love. Through those people we can come to know more about God. But it doesn't always work that way.
- Sometimes we separate ourselves from other people and let them down. If you have ever let anyone down, or did not recognize what they needed from you, drop your arms to your sides.
- Sometimes we say harmful things to others. If you have ever said anything to hurt another person, take a step backward.
- Sometimes we exclude others and make them feel unwanted. If you have ever made anyone feel left out of a group, take another step backward.
- Sometimes we say things that are not true. We deny making a mistake, or we are afraid to tell somebody something. If you have ever done that, turn and face away from the center of the circle.
- Sometimes we pretend not to see the needs of other people. Our hearts become hard as stone. If there have been times when you've ignored the needs of others, close your eyes and keep them closed.
- But we know that we need one another, and in our hearts, we know the things we must do to build the significant relationships in our lives. If you have ever helped someone who had a need, turn around to the center of the circle.
- We know it is important to listen to people and recognize their needs. If you have ever taken the time to listen to someone who had a problem, take one step in.

Catholic Faith Handbook connections

Use the "Prayer of Saint Francis," from pages 384–385 of the *CFH,* as a closing prayer. You might also use it as a reflection exercise, asking the young people to think of friends or acquaintances to whom each line applies.

Mediaconnections

◆ Compare the guidelines for building healthy friendships found in the Scriptures with those found in the popular media. Conduct the "Scripture search" activity in the Live It section of this chapter. Also choose a contemporary song on relationships, a magazine article on being a friend, or advertising slogans that use relationships as their gimmick. Discuss the results of the comparison.

◆ Check out *www.textweek.com*, *www.teachwithmovies.org*, and *www.hollywood jesus.com* for lists of movies on the session theme. Check out the ratings, the commentaries, and connections with the theme, and decide what is appropriate for your group.

Familyconnections

◆ Relationships within the family are likely to change significantly during adolescence. Sponsor an event where families can come together to discuss the changes, learn communication techniques, talk about relationship builders and relationship blockers, and just have fun.

◆ Suggest that the young people ask at least three older family members the following questions:

- We build people up when we welcome them and make them feel included. If you have ever made someone feel welcome and included, take another step into the circle.
- God asks us to tear down walls and forgive one another. If you have ever forgiven someone, open your eyes.
- God asks us to love one another. If you have ever let someone know in any way that—by your words or by your actions—you love them, put your arms on the shoulders of the people next to you.

3. Close with a sign of peace and a song about friendship.

Options and Actions

- **Scripture search.** Each of the following passages includes guidelines for building healthy relationships:
  ○ Sir. 6:5–17
  ○ Rom. 12:9–21
  ○ 1 Cor. 13:4–13
  ○ Col. 3:12–17

  Divide the participants into four small groups. Assign one citation to each group and ask each group to name the guidelines in its passage. Compile a list.

- **Creative friendship.** Relationships can become stagnant and even boring if friends stick to the same routine and activities. Brainstorm with the teens creative ideas for having fun and helping their relationships grow. In addition to recreational activities, be sure to cover shared service activities, hobbies, and the learning of new skills.

- **Love and friendship.** Read 1 Cor. 13:4–13. Explain that the descriptions of love in that passage are also rules for building healthy friendships. Discuss the benefits of putting those rules into practice and the consequences for not doing so. Also discuss how the rules help people move to deeper levels of friendship, even to intimacy.

- **Trust exercise.** Include a trust fall or a trust walk as part of the session. It would be particularly effective at the beginning of the session or at the point when you are presenting the differences between friendship and intimacy.

- **Helpful friends.** People may rely on their friends to help them through a tough time. Ask a mental-health professional to conduct a session on helping a friend who is depressed, suicidal, chemically dependent, being abused, or in a troubled relationship. The leader should focus on the signs to look for as well as how to get the person the help that he or she needs.
- **Jesus' relationships.** Explore the Gospels for characteristics of Jesus' relationship with others. Discuss what those characteristics tell us about Jesus' personality and style. You might also work with the young people to do a version of handout 1, "Circles of Relationships," using Jesus' relationships.
- **Friendship through the years.** Recruit a few pairs of friends of different ages and different genders. Lead an open discussion of the challenges and changes that friendships go through as people get older.
- **Life-giving relationships.** For a deeper exploration of the session topic, conduct the three-session minicourse titled "Life-giving Relationships," by Carole Goodwin, which is part of level 4 of the Horizons Program (Winona, MN: Saint Mary's Press, 1997). The course can be done as individual sessions or as a retreat. It is particularly appropriate for older adolescents.

◇ What are the three most important qualities of a healthy friendship?

◇ What are the three biggest obstacles to forming a good relationship?

◆ Suggest that each member of the family share her or his ideas about the qualities of a good friend. Compare the answers of young children, adolescents, parents, and grandparents.

JournalACTIVITIES

◆ Name three or four ideas to improve the quality of the relationships in your life. How will you implement those ideas?

◆ Keep track of the guidelines for building healthy friendships that you experience from others and that you put into practice yourself. Also keep track of relationship blockers and how you might counteract them.

Circles of Relationships

Write the names of the people in your life in the circles that represent their relationships with you.

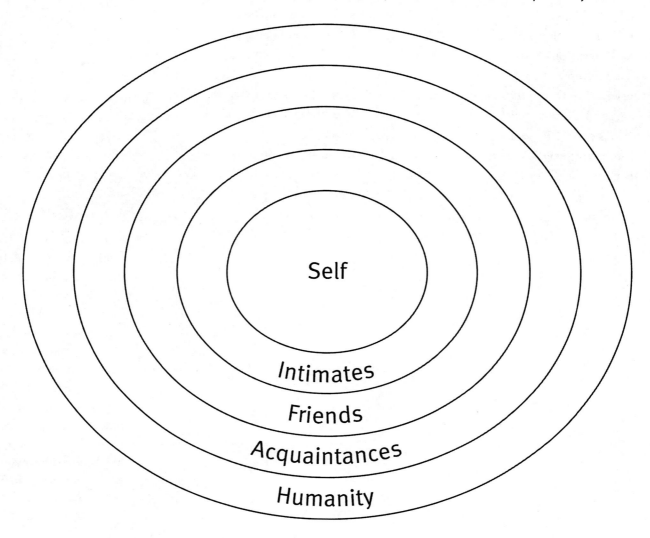

In which circles do you spend most of your time and energy?

In which circles do you need to spend more time and give more energy?

What does this analysis tell you about the relationships in your life?

3 Made in God's Image

Overview

Many adolescents experience times of shaky self-esteem. Some have difficulty establishing a positive self-image in the first place. Some of those feelings come from making one's self-image dependent on future events or comparing oneself to media stereotypes.

This session invites the young people to name the ways they make a difference in the world as children of God and parts of God's plan for the universe. It also encourages them to analyze the negative messages they get from the media and our culture. The session closes with a reading of Psalm 139, the ultimate statement of God's profound love and care for each of us.

Outcomes

- The participants will name the positive attributes that make them unique.
- The participants will critique negative messages from the media and our culture.
- The participants will select strategies and messages that honor them as persons made in God's image.

Background Reading

- Scriptural connections: Gen. 1:1—2:4 (the stories of Creation), Psalm 8 (divine majesty and human dignity), Matt. 5:13–16 (salt of the earth, light of the world), 2 Cor. 5:1–5 (The body is a temporary dwelling.)
- *Catholic Youth Bible* article connections: "In God's Image" (Gen. 1:26–27), "It's What's Inside That Counts" (2 Cor. 5:1–5)

Study It

Core Session:
Made in God's Image
(60 minutes)

- Focusing:
  Making a List and
  Checking It Twice
  (15 minutes)
- Presentation
  and Discussion:
  The Ifs and Whens of Life
  (20 minutes)
- Small-Group Discussion:
  Critiquing the Culture
  (20 minutes)
- Wrap-Up:
  Sentence Starters
  (5 minutes)

Pray It

- I'd Like the World
  to Know
  (15 minutes)

Live It

- It's what's inside
- Ad campaign
- A matter of pride
- Critiquing children's
  programming
- Just do it!
- Guided meditation
- I'd like the parish to know

Core Session:
Made in God's Image (60 minutes)

Preparation

- Gather the following items:
  - ☐ journals or blank paper
  - ☐ pens or pencils
  - ☐ small index cards or pieces of paper
  - ☐ newsprint
  - ☐ markers
  - ☐ masking tape
  - ☐ a *Catholic Youth Bible* or other Bible

Focusing: Making a List and Checking It Twice (15 minutes)

1. Tell the young people to take out their journals, or give each participant three sheets of blank paper and a pen or pencil. Explain that each person is to spend about 3 minutes making a list on one sheet of paper all the ways he or she is unlike anyone else. The teens are to list the things about themselves that are different, that separate them from others, and that make them distinct from everyone else. The items on the list can be positive or negative. Encourage the young people to refrain from analyzing or reflecting on the list. They should work as quickly as they can—silently and on their own.

2. Make the following points in your own words:

- The words *different* and *unique* have contrasting connotations in general usage. For some people, the word *different* has a negative connotation. It means that a person is separated from everyone else; the person possesses traits or characteristics that others do not have and probably would not want.

- The word *unique* puts a different slant on things. Many people interpret the word in a positive way. It might include gifts that make a person special or attributes and qualities that make a person worthwhile and lovable.

3. Explain to the young people that they are to make two columns on the second sheet of paper. One column should be headed "Different" and the other "Unique." Each person is to review the list she or he created and write each item from that list under one of the two headings, keeping in mind the different connotations of the two words. Allow about 3 minutes to complete the task.

4. Lead a brief large-group discussion of the following questions. Assure the young people that they do not have to share specific items from their lists.
- Why might two people put the same item in different categories?
- Why do some people feel "different," and others feel "unique"?
- What factors affect a person's self-image?

5. Invite the participants to make one final list of ten good qualities or characteristics about themselves. Again, allow about 3 minutes for the task. When everyone is finished, comment that their completed lists demonstrates that they are valuable, capable, and good people. Just the fact that they are human beings created by God makes them so. However, sometimes the eyes of the world are out of focus, which may affect how some people feel about themselves.

Presentation and Discussion: The Ifs and Whens of Life (20 minutes)

1. Make the following comments in your own words:
- Many people damage their self-esteem by fantasizing about an ideal future or state that results from their becoming or accomplishing something. These fantasies usually begin with statements like "If only I could . . ." and "When I get . . ."
- Although setting goals and planning ahead are positive things, an excessive focus on some ideal state can blind people to loving themselves unconditionally in the present. Some examples of the "If and When" syndrome follow:
  - If only I were better at math, I would get into a better college.
  - When I get more money, I'm going to buy a car that people will notice.
  - If only I had a boyfriend (girlfriend), I wouldn't feel so alone.
  - If only I could lose twenty pounds, I would be happy.
  - When I'm on my own, I'll spend my money the way I want to.
- Often when people focus on something they lack, they are missing the giftedness of another part of life. The person who concentrates on some future "when" may be missing the things that make him or her happy in the present. The people who long to be something they are not may neglect to value their strongest qualities.

TryThis

Divide the young people into small groups. Divide the cards equally among the groups. Suggest that the participants come up with a positive focus for each of the statements. Share with the large group as time allows.

VARIATION:
Gender Groups

Do this exercise in gender groups. Compare the "If only . . ." and "When I . . ." statements, and discuss the differences between the boys' and girls' statements.

2. Ask the young people to think about some of the "If only . . ." and "When I . . ." statements that they hold on to. While they are doing so, give each person an index card or a small piece of paper. Tell the young people to write a statement or two on the card. They are not to write their name on it.

3. Collect the statements and randomly read a few of them aloud. Solicit feedback from the participants on how the author might focus on a positive reality in her or his life. For example, if someone wrote, "If only I had a boyfriend, I wouldn't feel so alone," the group might suggest that the person focus on her friends of both genders and think about ways to develop deeper friendships with them.

Small-Group Discussion: Critiquing the Culture (20 minutes)

1. Divide the young people into small groups, and give each group a sheet of newsprint and some markers. Make the following comments in your own words:

- Messages from the media and our culture pose constant threats to a young person's self-esteem. Those messages are rarely direct, which in some ways makes them more harmful.
- The messages present ideals. We see strikingly beautiful young women at parties where beer flows freely, fast cars full of happy people headed to the beach, perfect bodies at the gym, and close friendships that are more a factor of the brand of jeans two people wear than of their soul connection. Amid all those ideals, being a normal, happy, and good human being can seem insufficient.
- By critiquing such messages, we can go beneath the surface and come closer to the truth. For example, by recognizing the message of a commercial that shows people having fun because everyone is wearing the right jeans, we can acknowledge that it is the people—each one unique and special—who make a gathering fun.

2. Explain that each group is to create a list called "The Top Five Media Messages We'd Like to Delete." The contents of the list should be commercials, advertisements, and story lines that contribute to low self-esteem. They should concentrate on images, TV shows, or ads that particularly affect young people. Candidates for the list might include messages that do any of the following things:

- equate a person's value with possessions, looks, and so forth
- foster "If only . . ." or "When I . . ." thinking
- present ideals designed to make normal people feel inferior

TryThis

Gather a variety of used magazines, preferably those that are aimed at teens and young adults. Distribute them among the small groups. Direct the participants to find ads that reflect the items on their lists.

Allow about 10 minutes for the small groups to complete their lists. Invite each group to share its list with everyone, and then post it. Solicit observations from the young people about the content of the lists.

Wrap-Up: Sentence Starters (5 minutes)

Pose each of the following sentence starters, and invite the young people to call out brief answers. Allow just 1 minute for responses to each sentence starter.

- I learned that . . .
- I still have questions about . . .
- I will use what I have learned in the coming week by . . .

Emphasize that each of us is a precious creation of a loving God, willed into being by God for the purpose of completing the universe. Close by reading Ps. 139:1–14, a testament to the God who willed us into being. If you have time, use the prayer service that follows, "I'd Like the World to Know," which is built around Psalm 139.

I'd Like the World to Know (15 minutes)

Preparation

- Gather the following items
  - ❑ index cards
  - ❑ pens or pencils
  - ❑ a candle and matches
  - ❑ a recording of reflective music and the appropriate equipment (optional)
  - ❑ a *Catholic Youth Bible* or other Bible
  - ❑ a basket
- Recruit three readers and assign one of the following passages to each of them:
  - ○ Ps. 139:1–4
  - ○ Ps. 139:5–7
  - ○ Ps. 139:13–14

1. Give each person an index card and a pen or a pencil. Light the candle, and begin playing reflective music if it is available. Make the following comments in your own words:

those people want the world to know. Have each group present its summary statement, interspersed with the response from Ps. 139:14. Close with a reading of Ps. 139:1–14.

Familyconnections

◆ Suggest that families look at the ads in magazines and newspapers around the house, particularly those that are aimed at children and teens. In what ways do those ads foster self-esteem? In what ways do they destroy it?

◆ Suggest that families acknowledge events and accomplishments that often go unmarked, such as finishing a major project, a half birthday (six months after a birthday), participating in a school play or concert, getting braces on or off, or an exercise milestone. Family life is full of things to celebrate.

Mediaconnections

◆ Several so-called reality-based TV shows and sitcoms carry strong messages about what it means to be a man or a woman, what it takes to be successful, and what a human being in relationship is all about. From the perspective of the impact on self-esteem and the theology of Creation,

- Each of us is a precious child of God, created in God's image. No one exactly like us has ever existed before, nor will anyone exactly like us exist in the future. Each person is part of God's plan to complete the universe.

- It is difficult for some people to believe that their uniqueness is a good thing and an essential component in God's plan to complete the universe. Messages from our culture, the media, and other people in our lives lead us to believe that we must be, do things, have things, think, or look like everyone else in order to be good.

- The Scriptures tell us that everything God created is good. Over and over in the Book of Genesis, we hear God's words of approval: "and indeed, it was very good" (Gen. 1:31). The world needs to know of our goodness. And we need to believe in it ourselves.

2. Invite the young people to think about how they would complete this sentence: "Something I want the world to know about me is . . ." After a few minutes of reflection, invite them to write the sentence on the index card. Collect the index cards and place them in a basket near the candle.

3. Explain to the young people that they will read their peers' anonymous statements describing what they want the world to know about them. While others are reading, they are to close their eyes and listen carefully and prayerfully. These statements could be from anyone—a best friend, a stranger, a class leader, or a loner.

Distribute the cards randomly, and divide the group into three parts. Invite one third of the group to stand and read their cards, each person in turn. When all the statements have been read, proclaim Ps. 139:14: "I praise you, for I am fearfully and wonderfully made." The group should respond with the second half of the verse: "Wonderful are your works." Then invite the first reader to proclaim Ps. 139:1–4. Pass the basket around the first group and collect the cards that were read.

Follow the same process with the other two groups and the other two scriptural readings.

LIVE it!

Options and Actions

- **It's what's inside.** Use the *Catholic Youth Bible* article "It's What's Inside That Counts," near 2 Cor. 5:1–5, as a journal exercise or for sharing between partners.

- **Ad campaign.** Divide the young people into small groups of five or six. Direct the groups each to create and perform a 30-second commercial that helps teenagers value their own gifts and abilities, acknowledge that they are worthwhile and lovable, or refrain from negative comparisons.

- **A matter of pride.** Suggest that the teens keep a running list of things of which they are proud. The list might include skills, accomplishments, something they did to help someone else, qualities, good decisions, and so on.

- **Critiquing children's programming.** List a few popular television shows and movies that are aimed at children and young adolescents. Assign small groups of teens to watch each show and critique it from the perspective of how it builds or breaks down a child's self-esteem.

- **Just do it!** Perhaps the surest way to build confidence and self-esteem is to be involved in activities that make a difference. Involve the teens in service of all kinds. Research opportunities for learning new skills, and connect the young people with them. Recruit adult mentors who are active in the community, and pair them up with teens. Let the teens know about the Boy Scouts' Explorer program and about its community-service agencies.

- **Guided meditation.** Lead the young people through the meditation on self-esteem and accompanying activities in *Guided Meditations for Youth on Personal Themes,* by Jane E. Ayer (Winona, MN: Saint Mary's Press, 1995).

- **I'd like the parish to know.** Publish several "I'd like the world to know" statements in the parish bulletin or on the parish Web site each week. Highlight the accomplishments of youth and the gift they are to the parish and to the community.

critique one or more of those shows with the teens.

- ◆ Check out *www.textweek.com, www.teachwithmovies.org,* and *www.hollywoodjesus.com* for lists of movies on the themes of personal growth and integrity. Check out the ratings, the commentary, and connections to the theme, and decide what is appropriate for your group.

VARIATION:
Gender Groups

- ◆ Divide the group according to gender. Have each gender group discuss what it thinks are typical thoughts or ideas of the other sex in the following areas:
  - ◇ sex
  - ◇ the definition of success in life
  - ◇ money
  - ◇ relationships
  - ◇ the most important thing in life
  - ◇ the definition of a perfect member of the other sex

  Bring the groups together, and have each one report the results of the discussion, giving each group a chance to respond after each topic.

4 Dating Relationships

Overview

Whether teens date or not, the subject of dating is always before them. Dating relationships are the topic of TV shows, movies, magazine articles, living room conversations, and banter in high school cafeterias. Most young people have not given much thought to the purpose of dating and how the activity of dating relates to their future. The point of this session is to get the teens thinking about the topic in purposeful ways, so that they might avoid some of the pitfalls of relationships that move too fast or get stuck at a certain level, in which partners have different expectations, or that are hurtful. Throughout the session the young people are urged to think about what is emotionally appropriate and what will bring growth to a dating relationship and to the individuals who are involved in it.

Outcomes

◆ The participants will explore different stages of dating relationships.
◆ The participants will understand that increasing levels of emotional intimacy accompany deepening relationships.

Background Reading

◆ Scriptural connections: Sir. 6:5–17 (faithful friends), Sir. 11:1–9 (the deceptiveness of appearances), 1 Cor. 13:1–13 (the gift of love)
◆ *Catholic Youth Bible* article connections: "Friends, Old and New" (Sir. 9:10), "Loving Others" (1 Corinthians, chap. 13), "Understanding Love" (1 John 4:7–21)

Core Session:
Dating—the Basics (60 minutes)

Preparation
- Gather the following items:
  - ❏ copies of handout 2, "Guess Test," one for each participant
  - ❏ pens or pencils
  - ❏ newsprint
  - ❏ markers
  - ❏ masking tape
  - ❏ blank paper
- On one sheet of newsprint, draw a ladder with ten rungs.
- List the following phrases on another sheet of newsprint:
  - ○ hanging out together
  - ○ group dating
  - ○ individual dating
  - ○ going steady
  - ○ engagement
  - ○ marriage
- Write each of the following sentence starters on a separate sheet of newsprint:
  - ○ We believe that young people who choose to date . . .
  - ○ We believe that dating relationships should . . .
  - ○ We believe that young people who date should not be pressured to . . .
  - ○ We believe that God calls all those who choose to date to . . .

Focusing: Guess Test (10 minutes)

1. Divide the young people into pairs, partnering teens of different genders if possible. Give each person a copy of handout 2, "Guess Test," and a pen or a pencil. Explain that they are to write in each blank the name of the person in their pair to whom they believe the statement applies *most accurately.* That is, they should write their own name or their partner's name after each statement. They should do this quickly and without talking to their partner or anyone else. Allow 3 or 4 minutes for this task.

2. Direct the pairs to score their "guess tests" by giving themselves 10 points for each correct guess. Invite them to share their scores and to discuss the results with each other, and with the large group if time allows.

TryThis

Add the following questions to the discussion at the end of the focusing activity:
◆ Why do people date?
◆ What rules about dating have you learned from older siblings and friends?

VARIATION:
Gender Groups

Do the brainstorming exercise, in step 1, in gender groups. Discuss the similarities and differences between the responses from the girls' group and the boys' group.

TryThis

Instead of drawing a ladder on newsprint, create one on the floor with masking tape. Make four signs for the levels of relationship, and place them on the appropriate rungs as directed.

3. Ask the young people how this activity is like dating. The similarities might include these observations:
• We may or may not know the person when we begin dating.
• We try to find common interests.
• We learn more about the other person.
• We sometimes judge by appearances.
• We sometimes make assumptions.

(This activity is adapted from Michael Theisen, *Dating and Love*, p. 20.)

Discussion: The Ideal Date (10 minutes)

1. Explain that there is no timeline for dating. Some people express an interest in dating early in their teen years. Others may not feel ready until they are older. No matter when a person begins dating, one of the biggest steps in dating is finding the right person. To take that first step, it is helpful for a young person to know his or her own expectations of a dating partner.

Divide the participants into small groups of four or five. Give each group a sheet of newsprint and markers. Have each group brainstorm a list of desirable qualities in a dating partner.

2. Instruct the groups to place an asterisk by the top five qualities they want in a future spouse. This step may take some simple voting by group members, but stress that they should not take too long in coming to a decision.

Ask the groups to post their lists, and allow a short time for the teens to review the results.

(This activity is adapted from Michael Theisen, *Dating and Love*, pp. 20–21.)

Presentation and Discussion: Looking for Love (25 minutes)

1. Display the ladder and the list of phrases describing dating levels that you created before the session. Make the following points:
• When one is dating, it is helpful to have a sense of the purpose and the goals of each level of a relationship so that one can keep expectations and commitments in line with each level.
• For example, one should not expect deep personal sharing from a partner on a first date. Conversely, if two people have been dating for some time and they are not sharing at a deep level, it is an indication that the relationship is stuck.

2. Write the phrase "Testing the Waters" on the first rung of the ladder, and then offer the following comments:
• In the beginning of a dating relationship, people experience a testing of the waters that might last through several dates. During that time each

person checks out the other, looking for shared interests, attractions, faults, warning signals, good feelings, and so on. The level of emotional intimacy is low.

- This testing level is an important step on the relational ladder because it helps us define what we want in a dating partner (and perhaps eventually in a spouse). Testing the waters is a time to decide if a person matches our expectations, interests, and values.

3. Ask the young people what type of dating relationship from those listed on the newsprint is appropriate at this level. Allow the teens to offer their ideas. Affirm the fact that hanging out, group dating, and individual dating are the best ways to achieve the goals of this level.

Write the word "Infatuation" on the fourth rung of the ladder. Explain the following ideas:

- This step is sometimes referred to as falling in love. At least in the early stages of infatuation, it is probably more proper to refer to it as falling in like, because true love is not likely at this point.

4. Ask the teens to call out words and phrases that they associate with this stage. Responses might include sweaty palms, constant thoughts, long phone calls, a churning stomach, and so forth. Then offer the following comments:

- The goal of this stage is to find out if the initial attraction goes deeper than just the surface. During this stage, partners find out more about each other and engage in deeper levels of sharing and emotional intimacy.
- If two people do not venture further up the relationship ladder, the relationship eventually tires out and ends—sometimes painfully.
- Relationships must grow and stretch if they are to flourish. Many relationships get stuck at the infatuation stage.

5. Ask the young people which types of relationships are appropriate to this level of intimacy. Group dating and individual dating are most suitable in the early stages. Going steady might be appropriate as the relationship moves up the rungs.

Write the words "Committed Friendship" on the seventh rung. Ask the young people to describe the characteristics of a relationship at this stage. Then note the following ideas:

- Every growing relationship must strive for this level. Deep friendship is marked by respect for each other, enjoyment of each other's company, time spent together in meaningful ways, common interests, and open and honest sharing.

6. Once again, ask the young people which type of relationship is most suitable at this stage. Going steady is typical for two people at this stage, though as they progress up the ladder, they may find themselves thinking and talking about becoming engaged.

Write the word "Love" on the tenth rung. Invite the young people to define the word as they understand it. After they share their thoughts, offer this explanation:

- The word *love* defines a committed, long-term, caring relationship. It can apply to many types of relationships: parent-child, God-person, and same-gender or mixed-gender relationships.

7. Ask the teens to identify actions and attitudes that characterize the love stage of a relationship, such as a willingness to work through conflicts, mutual respect, unselfishness, and forgiveness. Make the following comments:

- Love is a level of permanence and commitment that offers each partner a sense of security and trust. At this stage both people are highly invested in the relationship and are committed to sharing each other's joys and working through difficulties.
- This stage requires a high degree of emotional intimacy from both partners.

8. Ask the young people again to choose the type of relationships appropriate to this stage of emotional intimacy. Engagement and eventually marriage are right for two people at this stage. Then make these comments:

- Each rung on the ladder includes all the rungs below it. This means that it is possible—even necessary—for a love relationship to include both friendship and infatuation. A marriage that is not based on committed friendship and authentic love is likely to fail.
- Each stage might include many levels. For example, infatuation might be mild at first and then intensify as it progresses up the ladder, resulting in committed friendship.
- Though we are focused on dating relationships in this discussion, these stages can apply to all relationships. The dynamics of and activities within a relationship may change, depending on who is involved, but the stages and the fundamental qualities of each stage remain the same.

9. Offer the following questions for discussion:

- Do most young people confuse infatuation with love? with friendship? Why or why not?
- Is it possible for two people who are dating to be at different rungs on the ladder? If so, what is likely to happen?
- Which rung on the ladder, do you think, is achieved by most dating relationships among young people?

(This activity is adapted from Michael Theisen, *Dating and Love,* pp. 22–23.)

Discussion: A Dating Creed (15 minutes)

1. Divide the young people into small groups of four or five people. Give each group four sheets of blank paper and markers. Post the sentence starters that you listed on newsprint.

Explain that the young people are to discuss each sentence starter as a group, and then finish the statement. They are to write the completion on a sheet of paper and attach it to the newsprint. Allow about 10 minutes for the groups to work.

2. When all the statements have been posted, invite the participants to read them aloud. You may want to have four individuals read them, have four groups read them, or alternate between boys and girls.

3. Conclude the session by reiterating that whether they are currently dating or they have no plans to do so for a while, it is helpful to keep all that they talked about in this session in mind so that dating will be a true period of growth for themselves and for their relationships.

Dating Friends (20 minutes)

Preparation

- Gather the following items:
  - ❑ a candle and matches, a cross, and a basket
  - ❑ *Catholic Youth Bible*s or other Bibles, one for each participant
  - ❑ index cards
  - ❑ pens or pencils
  - ❑ a recording of a popular song about friendship and the appropriate equipment (optional)
- Set up a prayer table with a candle, a cross, and a basket.
- Write the following citations on separate index cards, repeating them so you have one card for every participant:
  - ○ Sir. 5:9–15
  - ○ Sir. 6:5–12
  - ○ Sir. 6:13–18
  - ○ Sir. 9:10–16
  - ○ Sir. 11:1–6
  - ○ Sir. 11:7–10
  - ○ Sir. 15:11–20
  - ○ Sir. 22:19–26

TryThis

- ◆ If time is limited, assign each group one sentence starter, and ask the members of the group to write two or three statements to finish it.
- ◆ Instead of doing a group activity, use the sentence starters as a reflection activity. Ask for volunteers to share their statements with the group, or compile the statements and send them to the young people.

TryThis

◆ Instead of using the index-card activity, engage the teens in a process of *lectio divina,* using one of the passages cited for reflection. For a discussion of *lectio divina,* check out the session titled "Praying with the Sacred Scriptures," found in the Total Faith manual *Catechetical Sessions for Prayer and Liturgy. The Catholic Faith Handbook for Youth* also includes a description of the process on pages 337–339.

◆ If your group is large, you are likely to have repeated verses. After each verse is read, invite anyone who wrote the same verse to add their card to the basket.

Familyconnections

◆ Dating stories from different generations are likely to be of interest to teens. Encourage them to talk to their parents, grandparents, and other relatives about their

1. Gather the young people in the prayer space. Make the following comments in your own words:

- The most successful dating partners are the ones who are also good friends. Ultimately two people who marry must also be close friends for the marriage to work. The rules for building a healthy dating relationship are the same as those for building a strong friendship.
- The Book of Sirach includes many guidelines for building and maintaining God-centered relationships. It was written by a wise teacher and translated by his grandson, who found the advice full of wisdom and just as applicable to his own life as it was to his grandfather's.

2. Give each young person a Bible, an index card, and a pen or pencil. Tell the young people to look up the passages cited on their index cards, read them, and write on their cards one verse from the cited passage that they believe everyone who is or will be involved in a dating relationship needs to hear. It should be a verse that they believe is critical to maintaining a relationship.

Light the candle. Invite the young people to hold up their Bibles as you read the following prayer; then allow about 5 minutes for reflection:

Open our mind to receive your word.
Open our lips to speak of your goodness.
Open our heart to share your love.

3. Invite each person in turn to share her or his piece of wisdom, and then to place the card in the basket on the prayer table. When everyone has shared their verse, lead the group in the formula used during the liturgy of the word at Mass: Draw three crosses while speaking these words: "May the word of God be in my mind, on my lips, and in my heart."

Close with a recording of a song on the theme of friendship, if you chose one before the session, or with an improvised prayer.

Options and Actions

- **Why do they always . . . ?** If you use the "Gender Groups" variation of dividing by gender for "The Ideal Date" activity, consider this: After the groups share their lists of desirable qualities in a dating partner, ask them to each develop a list of five questions they wish to ask the other gender. Instruct them to write the questions on newsprint, leaving space for answers. Exchange the newsprint sheets, and allow time for each gender group to answer the questions. Bring the groups together to share and discuss the answers.

- **Scriptural relationships.** Divide the young people into small groups, and assign one of the following passages to each group. Instruct the groups to decide which rung of the ladder the relationship described in the passage is at or the passage applies to, offering reasons for their answer.
  - Judg. 16:4–21
  - Ruth 1:11–18
  - 2 Sam. 11:2–5
  - Song of Sol. 1:2–4, 2:1–6
  - Sir. 6:5–16
  - John 15:9–15
  - 1 Cor. 13:1–8
- **The dating game.** Divide the teens into gender groups. Ask each group to write questions about dating for the other gender to answer. Bring everyone together for discussion of the questions. You might conduct the discussion in the form of a popular game show, choosing three "bachelors" or "bachelorettes" to answer the questions.
- **CREATIVE dating.** Brainstorm creative things to do and places to go on a date in your area. Offer the acronym *CREATIVE* before beginning the brainstorming. Note that every suggestion should include the following qualities:
  - **C**reative
  - **R**espectful
  - **E**conomical
  - **A**ccessible
  - **T**ake positive risks
  - **I**nvolve your date in planning
  - **V**ibrant
  - **E**njoyable
- **Special blessings.** Use a special occasion such as prom season or Valentine's Day to offer a special blessing for young people who are in dating relationships.
- **Problem dates.** Some young people find themselves in dating relationships that are physically or emotionally hurtful. Spend time talking about abusive relationships and discussing warning signs, strategies for getting out of such relationships, and resources for dealing with traumas such as date rape. You might want to invite a social worker or mental-health professional to talk to the group about those issues.
- **Panel discussion.** Invite an engaged couple or a newly married couple, a couple that have been married for at least ten years, and an elderly

experiences of dating. Give the teens questions such as these to ask their elders:
  ◇ When did you start dating?
  ◇ What did you do on your first date?
  ◇ What was your funniest experience of dating?
  ◇ What was your most embarrassing moment on a date?

◆ Encourage parents to share with their teenagers the qualities that attracted them to their spouse when they were dating, and to explain why other dating relationships ended.

◆ Suggest that parents share with their teens some advice about dating, in a list titled "Things I learned while I was dating."

Mediaconnections

◆ Invite the young people to bring in popular music on the topic of relationships between men and women. Critique the lyrics from the perspective of Christian relationships. You might ask the following questions:
  ◇ What do the lyrics indicate is important in a dating relationship?
  ◇ Would you want to date someone who thought this way about you? Why or why not?

◆ Gather a variety of popular magazines that include articles on relationships. Discuss the attitudes toward dating and relationships that emerge in the articles.

◆ Suggest that the young people look for examples of healthy, Christ-centered relationships in the TV shows and movies they watch during the coming week or so. Discuss their findings at a future gathering.

Journal ACTIVITIES

◆ If you are currently dating, what has your dating experience been like thus far? What has been the most exciting part? the most difficult part?

◆ How are you being challenged to grow in your relationships with people of the other gender? How does this challenge make you feel?

◆ Create a biography and composite of the ideal dating partner for you. Include physical and personality characteristics as well as background and interests.

couple who have been married since they were young to participate in a panel discussion on dating. Encourage the teens to ask questions.

• **Reconciliation.** Conduct a sacramental celebration of Reconciliation, with emphasis on healing the brokenness and hurt that are often experienced by young people who have ended a relationship or who have gone too far sexually in a relationship.

• **Rules for dating.** Divide the young people into small groups. Have each group develop a list of ten rules for dating. Discuss the results. Then compile a comprehensive list of rules and share it with all the teens in the parish.

Guess Test

Decide whether each statement applies most accurately to you or to your partner, and write that person's name in the blank. Do not talk to your partner or anyone else.

1. the person who has the most siblings

   _____

2. the person who last saw a movie in a theater

   _____

3. the person who is taller

   _____

4. the person whose birthday is closest to today

   _____

5. the person who has moved most often

   _____

6. the person who has the least amount of money with her or him now

   _____

7. the person who has been a member of the parish the longest

   _____

8. the person who last ate fast food

   _____

Score: _____

5 Accepting and Honoring Others

Overview

Every human being is born with the same emotional needs. Those needs stay with us throughout our lives. During childhood, family usually fulfills our needs, but as we become adolescents, we look beyond the family to meet them. Here we encounter the challenges of a peer culture that holds self-preservation as a high value, often at tremendous emotional cost. We also encounter prevailing cultural prejudices that go far beyond the peer group. The point of this session is to raise awareness of emotional needs and the harm that is caused when people do not honor those needs in themselves and others. The result is often some expression of emotional abuse, which causes pain and frequently leads to the abuse of others. At the close of the session, the teens are invited to brainstorm ways to break the cycle of abuse.

Outcomes

◆ The participants will understand that all human beings share the same basic emotional needs.
◆ The participants will be challenged to let go of prejudices and stereotypes and to see that all people strive to be fully human.
◆ The participants will explore ways to counteract negative behaviors and attitudes.

Background Reading

◆ Scriptural connections: Rom. 12:9–21 (marks of a true Christian), Rom. 14:13–19 (Do not pass judgment on others.), Col. 3:12–15 (new life in Christ)
◆ *Catholic Youth Bible* article connections: "A Prayer Against Prejudice" (Joshua, chap. 2), "Seeing with God's Eyes" (John, chap. 9), "Becoming a Peacemaker" (Rom. 12:17–19), "A Real Love" (Rom. 13:8–10)

Core Session:
Being Fully Human (60 minutes)

Preparation

- Gather the following items:
  - ❏ a flip chart (optional)
  - ❏ markers
  - ❏ newsprint
  - ❏ a copy of resource 1, "The Next Time . . . , cut apart as scored
- For the reflection and discussion activity "Have You Ever . . . ?," you will need a room large enough for the teens to move around in freely.
- Write the following list of emotional needs on newsprint or on the board:
  - ○ the need for relationships with other people
  - ○ the need for appropriate touching and holding
  - ○ the need to belong and feel "one" with others
  - ○ the need to be different and separate
  - ○ the need to care for and help other people
  - ○ the need to feel worthwhile, valued, and admired
  - ○ the need for power in our relationships and in our life

Focusing: Media Miscues (5 minutes)

1. Invite the young people to name TV shows, news stories, and movies they have seen in the last week that included any of the following scenarios:

- bullying, teasing, or making fun of others
- people being excluded from a group
- stereotypes of women's or men's emotional behavior
- prejudice based on race, ethnicity, religion, or disability

2. Explain that negative attitudes toward others are pervasive in our society, and are accepted by some as normal behavior, as evidenced by the young people's experience of the media. Those attitudes often result in negative behaviors that are hurtful to others and to ourselves. The point of this session will be to look at what makes us fully human, that is, sharers in the humanity of Jesus.

Reflection and Discussion: Have You Ever . . . ? (25 minutes)

1. Gather the young people along one wall of the room. Explain that you will read a number of statements about experiences they may have had, and that at the end of each statement, you will give them instructions about what to do next. Encourage them to go through this exercise silently and reflectively, refraining from discussion until directed to talk.

Pose some of the following questions, based on the time you have available and the willingness of the group. Choose questions that are most appropriate for the age and experience level of the young people. You may want to add some questions of your own. Encourage the teens to be honest, and assure them that they will not be asked to share specifics about their situations.

When the teens are ready, begin with the following question:

- Have you ever felt discriminated against or looked down on because of your age?

Give the following directions, pausing after each one to give the teens a chance to move (if they choose to) and reflect. Insist on silence throughout the activity.

- If so, move to the other side of the room.
- Look at who is with you.
- Look across the room.
- Silently return to your starting point.

Use the same process for each subsequent question:

- Have you ever been hurt by someone who made fun of you for the way you look or for something you said or did?
- Have you ever wished your parents would pay a little more attention to you or say something to you that you really want to hear?
- Have you ever felt at a disadvantage because of your gender? Have you ever wanted to do or have something, but felt restricted because you are male or female?
- Have you ever worried about relationships within your family?
- Have you ever been bullied or teased to the point that you were scared, angry, or hurt?
- Have you ever been the victim of physical violence?
- Have you ever felt discriminated against because of the part of town you live in, your ethnicity, or your economic status?
- Have you ever felt really sad, but not told anyone about it?
- Have you ever helped someone who is younger or older than you, just because you wanted to?
- Have you ever felt looked down on or ridiculed because of your religious beliefs?

- Have you ever felt betrayed by a friend?
- Have you ever been a victim of stereotyping?
- Have you ever had a great dream that you would do something wonderful someday?
- Have you ever felt like crying, but held back because you thought people might make fun of you or because you would be embarrassed?
- Have you ever been fascinated by something you learned in school, but felt like you couldn't say anything because it wasn't cool?
- Have you ever wanted a hug from someone, but were afraid to ask for one?
- Have you ever done something you didn't want to do, just to fit in?
- Have you ever been sexually harassed by any means, including unwelcome comments about your body, and comments or jokes with sexual innuendos that made you feel uncomfortable?
- Have you ever felt that you were really good at something and would like the chance to prove it?
- Have you ever felt scared at a time when people expected you to be brave?

2. Gather the young people and invite them to share their experiences and observations about the exercise. Lead a discussion of the following questions; you may want to write the responses on a flip chart:
- What does this exercise tell us about people?
- What are some of the basic emotional needs that all human beings have?
- How do other people stand in the way of those needs being met?

Be sure that the following points emerge from the discussion:
- Everyone has had hurtful experiences of being put down, undervalued, made fun of, or emotionally abused.
- All people share the same emotional needs and have a right to have those needs met in a positive way.
- Acknowledging and respecting those needs is the key to understanding and honoring ourselves and others.

Presentation: Needs and Obstacles (10 minutes)

Display the list of emotional needs that you prepared before the session. Present the following points in your own words, referring to the list and adding illustrations and comments from the young people:
- Every human being has the same basic emotional needs. Those seven needs are common to all people, no matter where they live, what they look like, or what their age, gender, and background are. They were ordained in us at the moment of conception by our Creator, as they were ordained in every person who ever lived and every person who is yet to be. Having needs and expressing emotion are part of being fully human.
- Needs and wants are very different. A boy might tell his parents that he *needs* a new name-brand jacket that is popular with teens. But what he is

TryThis

Instead of inviting the teens to share their observations verbally, ask them to write three observations on a sheet of paper. Collect the papers and share them with the group anonymously.

VARIATION:
Gender Groups

Bullying takes different forms for each gender. We associate the classic image of bullying, including physical threats, challenges, and violence, with boys. The female form of bullying is usually expressed through exclusionary tactics such as forming cliques, in which one or two girls dominate the thinking of the group and exclude others. Sometimes this is referred to as the "queen bee" syndrome. Discuss those expressions of violence in gender groups, including the similarities and differences between the two expressions and ways to deal with them.

really saying is that he *wants* a new jacket so that he can feel like he belongs and is "one" with others. A girl might say she *needs* an A in a class. But what she may really be saying is that she *wants* an A because it will make her feel admired by others, worthwhile, and valued.

- Emotions and feelings are the result of our needs either being met or not being met.
  - A person might feel anger if she or he does not feel valuable.
  - A hug can give a person a feeling of joy, comfort, or happiness.
  - The fear of expressing sadness can make a person feel lonely.
  - Being part of a team can give a person a sense of security and belonging.
- What usually stands in the way of people getting their emotional needs met is other people. Stereotypes, prejudices, false assumptions, teasing, and bullying are ways that people dishonor and disrespect the humanness of one another.
- When people are not allowed to express their emotions and their needs, they deny a part of who they are. That denial often results in negative behaviors, and may have adverse effects on emotional health and on relationships. People who are hurt will often hurt other people. The cycle continues.
- The most wonderful thing a person can do for others is to allow them to express their emotional needs and feelings without fear of ridicule. The best thing a person can do for himself or herself is to find a caring friend or trusted adult with whom he or she can be totally honest and can express the full range of needs and emotions.

(This activity is adapted from Marilyn Kielbasa, *Finding Your Personal Style*, pp. 52–53.)

Small-Group Discussion: The Next Time . . . (20 minutes)

1. Divide the young people into groups of four or five people. Distribute segments of resource 1, "The Next Time . . . ," evenly among the groups, along with a sheet of newsprint and a marker for each statement. Explain that the groups are to offer advice to people who are facing difficult choices, using what they learned in the session.

Tell them to read each sentence starter and discuss as a group what advice they should give and some reasons for the advice. You may want to offer the following examples:

- The next time you feel sad but are hesitant to say anything, find a good friend or an adult that you trust and tell that person how you feel. Why? Because your feelings are real. They are part of who you are, and you need to acknowledge them.

Familyconnections

- Offer some of the "Have you ever . . . ?" statements to families for discussion. Also provide them with a copy of resource 1, "The Next Time . . . ," and encourage them to come up with ideas for countering actions and attitudes that are harmful or hurtful.
- Share the seven emotional needs with families, and suggest that they post the list in a central location.

- The next time someone shares an idea that you think is completely off-the-wall and really dumb, don't put the person down. Why? Just because you don't like the idea doesn't mean it's not a valid one; it just means that the two of you think differently. You both reflect God's creativity in some way.

2. Allow time for the groups to share their advice with one another. Affirm the concept that we must honor ourselves and one another, respect the needs of each person, challenge negative thinking, and work to eliminate the attitudes and behaviors that are harmful and hurtful. Only then can we attain the fullness of life of which Jesus speaks.

3. Close by reading Matt. 5:13–16, Jesus' words about being light for the world and salt for the earth, and comment that the only way to do that is to be light and salt for one another.

Pray It

Living as Peacemakers (15 minutes)

Preparation
- Gather the following items:
  - ❑ an assortment of magazines and newspapers
  - ❑ a *Catholic Youth Bible* or other Bible
  - ❑ a candle and matches
  - ❑ a recording of reflective music and the appropriate equipment (optional)
  - ❑ three copies of resource 2, "Prayer of a Peacemaker"
- Search the magazines and newspapers for pictures of as many different kinds of people as possible. Include people of various ages and races, of both genders, and in various styles of dress.
- Set up a prayer space with a Bible and a candle. Spread the pictures on the floor around the prayer space.
- Recruit three readers for the prayer on resource 2, and someone to proclaim Rom. 12:9–18.

1. Light the candle, and play reflective music in the background if you choose to do so. Invite the participants, including the four readers, to move quietly around the prayer space and study the different pictures. After a few minutes, ask the teens to silently sit near the image that is *least* like themselves, and to concentrate on it during the prayer.

Encourage them to address one need at a time in a more intentional way in their family life, and discuss how they can support others' needs in their work or school lives.

Spirit & Song connections
- ◆ "Go Make a Difference," by Steve Angrisano and Tom Tomaszek
- ◆ "We Gotta Love," by Tom Booth, Israel Houghton, and Matt Maher

Try This

Instead of gathering pictures before the session, provide a variety of magazines, and ask the teens to find pictures. You may want to direct the teens to find ones that meet certain criteria, such as these:
- ◆ a person who is most unlike you
- ◆ a person you would like to get to know better
- ◆ a person you would enjoy as a friend

◆ a person you would be afraid to encounter

Mediaconnections

◆ Check out *www.textweek. com, www.teachwithmovies. org,* and *www.hollywood jesus.com* for lists of movies on the session theme. Check out the ratings, the commentary, and the connections to the theme, and decide what is appropriate for your group.

◆ Sponsor a program on media awareness. In particular, look for examples of emotional violence such as bullying, berating, controlling, prejudice, racism, and sexism. You might also have high school teens lead a program on the topic for younger teens, focusing on how to stop the cycle.

JournalACTIVITIES

◆ Which of the seven emotional needs are not adequately met in your life? What ideas do you have for meeting those needs in a positive way?

◆ Who can you talk to about your struggles with some of those issues?

◆ If you've been a victim of emotional or physical bullying, teasing, exclusion, or prejudice, how did you handle those situations? What advice would you give to someone who is experiencing difficulties?

2. Lead the prayer as it is outlined in resource 2. Close by inviting the reader to proclaim Rom. 12:9–18.

(This activity is adapted from Gail Daniels Hassett, *Becoming a Peacemaker,* pp. 24–25.)

Options and Actions

- **Kids need to know.** Have the teens lead a series of programs for older children and young teens on honoring one another, meeting needs, respecting differences, and responding to difficult situations like bullying and cliques. A wonderful resource on this topic for their age-group is *Stick Up for Yourself: Every Kid's Guide to Personal Power and Positive Self-Esteem,* second edition, by Gershen Kaufman, Lev Raphael, and Pamela Espeland (Minneapolis: Free Spirit Publishing, 1999), and the accompanying leader's guide.

- **Needs posters.** Provide poster board and art materials. Have the young people create several posters of the seven emotional needs. Display them in places where people gather. You might also have the teens create bookmarks and miniposters to give to younger teens or to take home for their families.

- **Info night.** Invite a speaker on the topic of violence to address the teens. Direct the person to sensitize the young people to the full continuum of violence, from name-calling, verbal abuse, and bullying to the use of weapons.

- **Mediation training.** Check with local schools to see if they have a program to train young people in mediation skills. Invite a facilitator to share her or his experiences.

- **Seuss night.** Use the stories of Dr. Seuss that have social-justice themes to talk about prejudice and emotional violence. They include *The Lorax, The Butter Battle Book, The Sneetches,* and *Horton Hears a Who.* Encourage the teens to research Dr. Seuss's background and share his story.

- *Lectio divina.* Engage the teens in the *lectio divina* prayer form, using Psalm 139, a psalm about the intimate emotional relationship between God and us. A good resource for leading teens in this process is *Bringing Catholic Youth and the Bible Together,* edited by Brian Singer-Towns (Winona, MN: Saint Mary's Press, 2000), pages 68–77.

The Next Time . . .

The next time you are tempted to make fun of someone . . .

Why?

The next time you hear an off-color joke . . .

Why?

The next time you hesitate to tell someone how you feel . . .

Why?

The next time you think you are being discriminated against because of your age . . .

Why?

The next time your friends start to tease or bully someone . . .

Why?

The next time you feel excluded from a group . . .

Why?

The next time you have a wild idea to share . . .

Why?

The next time you think a stereotypical thought . . .

Why?

The next time you feel that you are being bullied . . .

Why?

The next time you feel pressure to be a certain way just because of your gender . . .

Why?

Prayer of a Peacemaker

Leader: We say we are Christians.

Reader 1:

We know we are all children of God.
We hear voices speaking in a symphony of languages.
We see a rainbow of hands reaching out to connect with one another.

Leader: We say we are Christians.

Reader 2:

We pray from hearts filled with experiences as male and female
young and old
poor and rich
from every corner of God's gift.

Leader: We say we are Christians.

Reader 3:

We are sons and daughters of God.
It is our faith that unites us.
It is our differences that enrich us.
It is our challenge to put aside our differences and live as Jesus taught.

Leader: Let us live as the Christians we say we are.

(This prayer is adapted from Gail Daniels Hassett, *Becoming a Peacemaker* [Winona, MN: Saint Mary's Press, 1996], pages 24–25, copyright © 1996 by Saint Mary's Press, all rights reserved.)

6 Choices and Decisions

Overview

Every day we are confronted with many decisions, big and small. Often we make decisions in a haphazard way, not considering all the facts, options, and consequences. Like adults, teens face many decisions. Some of those decisions are simple ones and are not life changing. Others are more significant, involving moral choices, life choices, or relationships. This session provides a process for making choices that if followed carefully, can help teens make choices that will lead to a holy, happy, and healthy life.

Outcomes

◆ The participants will learn a process for making decisions.
◆ The participants will apply the process to decisions they face.

Background Reading

◆ Scriptural connections: Psalm 63 (comfort and assurance in God's presence), Rom. 7:14–25 (the struggle between knowing and doing what is right), Col. 3:5–17 (the traits of a Christian)
◆ *Catholic Youth Bible* article connections: "Decide!" (Psalm 62), "Our Inner Struggle" (Rom. 7:14–25), "Conscience: God in the Gut" (1 Tim. 1:18–19), "Live in the Light" (1 John 1:5–10)

Study it!

Core Session:
Making Decisions for Life (60 minutes)

Preparation
- Gather the following items:
  - ☐ newsprint and markers
  - ☐ masking tape
  - ☐ copies of handout 3, "LISTENing for a Solution," one for each participant
  - ☐ copies of handout 4, "LISTENing in the Quiet," one for each participant
  - ☐ pens or pencils
  - ☐ a recording of reflective music and the appropriate equipment (optional)

Focusing: Daily Decisions (20 minutes)

1. Brainstorm with the young people a list of decisions that they frequently have to make. Some of the decisions may be simple ones—like deciding what to wear in the morning. Others are more complex and serious, like deciding what to do after high school. Allow about 2 minutes for brainstorming, and write all the answers on newsprint.

2. Divide the participants into small groups of four or five people and give each group a sheet of newsprint and some markers. On the brainstormed list highlight a number of situations that exemplify the kinds of decisions for which young people need a decision-making process. Tell the groups to choose one of the situations, and to name the steps they would go through to come up with a decision in that situation and then list the steps on newsprint. Allow about 10 minutes for this task.

3. Invite someone in each small group to present its decision-making process to the large group. After each presentation, post the small group's newsprint.

4. Gather the participants and discuss the following questions:
- What did you hear about the way people make decisions?
- Were there common elements in the approaches? If so, what were they?

TryThis

After the decision brainstorming activity, tell the teens to stand up and start walking north. The result is likely to be confusion. Once everyone has decided which way to go, give one of the teens a compass to determine which way is truly north. Briefly discuss the following questions:
- ◆ If you did not know exactly which direction is north, how did you determine which way to start walking? Were you correct?
- ◆ What does this exercise have to do with making decisions?

Comment on the importance of having a clear plan when one makes important decisions, like which direction to follow in life. If possible, provide everyone with a toy compass at the end of the session as a reminder of what they learned.

Presentation and Discussion: LISTENing for a Solution (25 minutes)

1. Distribute handout 3, "LISTENing for a Solution." Summarize the following points in your own words, adding comments from the participants and stories of your own as time allows:

- *LISTEN* is an acronym that describes a process for making decisions. The process is simple, is adaptable, and can be used by groups or individuals. In a simplified form, it can be used to make uncomplicated decisions, such as how to spend a free weekend or what cocurricular activities to pursue. In its complete form, the process can be used to make moral decisions and life choices. The acronym stands for the following steps:
  - **L**ook for the facts. Clearly define the situation, both internally and externally. What is the decision that needs to be made? Identify details that might influence how the situation could be resolved.
  - **I**magine possibilities. Brainstorm all the options. Consider the consequences. What are the advantages and disadvantages of each option? Be sure to include concrete factors as well as moral and value concerns.
  - **S**eek insight beyond your own. Look for help from your family, your friends, and wise people you trust. If you are making a moral or ethical decision, find out what Jesus and the Church teach about the issue.
  - **T**urn inward. Examine your own feelings and insights from your experiences, motives, and values. What might God be calling forth in you? What does your conscience tell you? What is your inner reality?
  - **E**xpect God's help. Believe that God is present in your life, especially in your honest attempts to seek the truth. If the decision significantly affects your ability to grow into a holy, healthy, and happy adult, turn to God in prayer with an attitude of openness.
  - **N**ame your decision. Verbalize or write it. Sometimes, naming the decision means postponing it until you can do more thinking or gather more information. Identify the reason for the delay.
- Think of the LISTEN process as a pie cut into six pieces. Sometimes the pieces come out neat and separate when lifted from the pan, like a cheesecake. Most of the time, however, it is like a juicy, messy blueberry pie: when you try to lift out one of the pieces, they all run together.

2. Refer to the list of decisions generated at the beginning of the session. Discuss with the young people the following questions:

- For what kinds of decisions would the whole LISTEN process be helpful? (moral decisions, life-changing decisions)
- How could you modify the process for simple decisions?
- Compare the LISTEN process with the process that your group identified. What do you find in common? What is missing?

TryThis

In step 2, assign each small group a decision from the list that is significant to teens because of its life impact or moral implications. You may have to brainstorm more situations if the ones on the list are not sufficient. Have each small group apply the LISTEN process to its assigned situation. Explain that the groups do not have to come up with a decision, but should simply identify the specific elements of the process.

(This activity is adapted from Julia Ahlers, Barbara Allaire, and Carl Koch, *Growing in Christian Morality,* pp. 78–82.)

Reflection: LISTENing in the Quiet (15 minutes)

1. Distribute handout 4, "LISTENing in the Quiet," and pens or pencils. Invite the teens to think of a decision they are now facing. You may want to specify a category, such as a moral decision, a life-direction decision, a relationship decision, or a self-development decision. Announce that in the next few minutes, they will have an opportunity to apply the LISTEN process to their own situations. Encourage them to find a place where they can be alone with their thoughts and not be distracted by others. Allow about 10 minutes for them to work through handout 4. Caution the participants to take their time to simply think through the steps and jot down a few notes. They can complete the process when they have more time. Play reflective music in the background while they work, if you so desire.

2. Comment on the importance of using an intentional decision-making process when wrestling with the big decisions of life. An abbreviated form of the process is helpful even when the decisions are not life altering but still require careful thought. Using the process for less significant decisions can help develop the ability and readiness to tackle big decisions that will come along.

3. Close by reading Matt. 7:7–8, an invitation to ask for help and seek the truth. Or if time allows, do the prayer service that follows, "A Piece of the Puzzle."

A Piece of the Puzzle (15 minutes)

Preparation
- Gather the following items:
  - ❑ a permanent marker
  - ❑ blank jigsaw puzzle pieces, preferably large ones, like those in a children's puzzle, one for each participant
  - ❑ a candle, a cross, and other symbols of Christian worship
  - ❑ a basket or a bowl
  - ❑ a *Catholic Youth Bible* or other Bible
  - ❑ pens or pencils

TryThis

In step 1, assign a partner to each person. Have the pairs discuss the decision-making process and handout 4, sharing only if they are comfortable doing so. Encourage them to name their next steps and commit to a specific action.

❏ a recording of reflective music and the appropriate equipment (optional)

• With a permanent marker, write the citation "Matthew 7:7–8" on the front of every puzzle piece.

• Create a prayer space with a candle, a cross, and other symbols of Christian worship. Place the puzzle pieces in a basket or a bowl, and add the container to the prayer space.

• Recruit a volunteer to read Matt. 7:7–8.

1. Gather the young people around the prayer space, and give each one a pen or a pencil. Pass the basket of puzzle pieces around the group, and tell the teens to each take one puzzle piece in silence. As they are doing so, make the following comments in your own words:

• Sometimes life feels like a puzzle. We spend most of our time trying to put together the pieces so that everything fits. The puzzling pieces of life are things like these:

  ○ I like three sports, but only have time for one. Which should I choose?

  ○ Do I want to go to college? What major should I choose?

  ○ Some of my friends are going to a party this weekend. Should I go with them? I know there's going to be alcohol.

• All those uncertainties are a part of the puzzle of life. Even great saints had to struggle. Saint Paul struggled with what he called a "thorn . . . in the flesh" (2 Cor. 12:7).

2. Direct the teens to write on the backs of their puzzle pieces a word or two that describes a big decision they are facing. Remind them of the reflection paper they completed (handout 4), and encourage them to write one of the situations from that reflection on their puzzle pieces.

3. After a few minutes, continue with the following comments:

• We do not know what Paul's thorn was, but we know that he begged God three times to take it away. God said to him, "My grace is sufficient for you, for power is made perfect in weakness" (2 Cor. 12:9).

• God's grace is all we need. No matter what decisions we face, what choices we have to make, what problems we have to solve, God will get us through. And the good news is that God's grace is already there—in every piece of our lives. We just need to recognize it.

4. Ask the reader to proclaim Matt. 7:7–8. Encourage the young people to take their puzzle pieces home. Point out that the citation for the scriptural passage they just heard is on the front of the piece. Suggest that they read the passage when they feel anxious about a decision they are facing.

(This activity is adapted from Lisa-Marie Calderone-Stewart, *Prayer Works for Teens Book 4*, pp. 32–34.)

Options and Actions

- **Gospel decisions.** Divide the teens into small groups, assign one of the following passages to each group, and communicate the story line indicated in parentheses:
  - Matt. 1:18–25 (Joseph takes Mary as his wife.)
  - Matt. 4:18–22 (The disciples agree to follow Jesus.)
  - Mark 10:17–22 (The rich man approaches Jesus and then turns away.)
  - Mark 14:66–72 (Peter denies Jesus.)
  - Luke 1:26–38 (Mary says yes to God.)
  - Luke 15:11–24 (The prodigal son leaves, then returns.)
  - John 2:1–12 (Jesus performs his first miracle at Cana.)
  - John 3:1–16, 7:45–52 (Nicodemus visits Jesus.)

  Explain to the groups that their task is to discuss the decision the person in the story had to make and to apply the LISTEN process to the story. They will have to create some details, such as the feelings of the main characters or some of the circumstances.
- **Seek and you shall find.** Gather a variety of books from the Where's Waldo? or I Spy series. Begin the session by having the young people find Waldo or an identified object. Connect the activity to the decision-making process by noting that the best decision is not always clear. Just as it takes work to find a picture, it takes careful thought to come to a good decision.
- **Case studies.** Several collections of case studies are available for practice in making moral decisions. Use one to help the teens get comfortable using the LISTEN model. One such resource is *Growing in Christian Morality: Student Casebook,* by Kathleen Crawford Hodapp (Winona, MN: Saint Mary's Press, 2002).
- **Mission statements.** To make a good decision about the direction of one's life, it is important to have a goal. Give the young people an opportunity to develop their own mission statements. *The Seven Habits of Highly Effective Teens: The Ultimate Teenage Success Guide,* by Sean Covey (New York: Simon and Schuster, 1998), is a helpful resource.
- **Creative visualization.** Creatively visualizing one's past and present from the perspective of one's future can be a helpful tool in making life decisions. One can do this by asking the question, "How do I want to be remembered?" Lead the teens in a reflection using the following or similar questions:

Familyconnections

- ◆ Share handout 3, "LIS-TENing for a Solution," with parents. Encourage them to talk with their teens about decisions the teens face and to offer support and encouragement. Suggest that they use the LISTEN model to make decisions that affect the entire family.
- ◆ Suggest that the teens ask older members of their families how they made important decisions in their lives, such as decisions about vocation, career, moral challenges, relationships, or faith.
- ◆ *The Power of Discernment: Helping Your Teen Hear God's Voice Within,* by Maggie Pike (Winona, MN: Saint Mary's Press, 2003), is a practical resource for parents to use in helping their teens create a healthy life from healthy choices. The book offers a method of discernment for dealing with issues such as peer pressure, friends, sexuality, and family well-being.

Mediaconnections

- ◆ Suggest that the young people view their favorite television shows or movies from the perspective of making decisions. How do the characters make important decisions? What factors do they consider? What is missing from the process?

◆ Check out *www.textweek. com, www.teachwith movies.org,* and *www. hollywoodjesus.com* for lists of movies on the session theme. Check out the ratings, the commentary, and the connections to the theme, and decide what is appropriate for your group.

VARIATION:
Gender Groups

Whenever small groups are used in this session, group the teens according to gender. As part of the ensuing discussion, note the differences in the results of the groups' work. For example, the small groups may come up with entirely different decision-making processes in the first activity, a result that may be attributed partly to gender differences.

Journal**ACTIVITIES**

◆ What decisions did you make this week that you are confident were made carefully and prayerfully?

◆ Describe a time when you made a wrong choice. What would you do differently now?

◆ What major decisions do you face in the near future?

○ What will your family members say about you as a member of a family?

○ What kind of job will you have? How will you make a contribution to the world through that job?

○ What will your colleagues say about you as a worker?

○ What will your neighbors say about you as a citizen and a member of the community?

○ In what causes will you be active? What service will you provide?

○ What will the members of your church say about you? In what parish activities will you be involved? How important will your faith be?

○ Sum up your life in a sentence or two. What will you be all about? For what will you be remembered? How will you live your life?

• **Reflecting on choices.** Use one of the following articles from *The Catholic Youth Bible* as a basis for reflection:

○ "You Shall Be Holy" (Leviticus, chaps. 19–20)

○ "Reaping the Whirlwind" (Hos. 8:7)

• **Gifts of the Spirit.** Review with the teens the seven gifts of the Holy Spirit: wisdom, knowledge, understanding, right judgment, awe, reverence, and courage. Discuss which gifts are most useful at each step of the LISTEN process.

• **Decision versus discernment.** If you are working with older teens, discuss the differences between making a decision and entering a process of discernment, which is defined as the "evaluation of the presence or absence of God, or the presence of an evil spirit, in making decisions and carrying them out" (Richard P. McBrien, *HarperCollins Encyclopedia of Catholicism,* p. 419). *The Catholic Faith Handbook for Youth* includes a relevant piece in the Live It article "Top Ten Ways for Seeking God's Will," found in chapter 36, "The Lord's Prayer: God's Glory." Also, discernment is the main topic of the opening chapters of *An Inside Look: A Leader's Guide to the Vocations Series,* by Clare vanBrandwijk (Winona, MN: Saint Mary's Press, 2002).

• **Wrapping up the session.** Use the following questions to close the session. They can be posed in large- or small-group discussions, or as questions for journal writing.

○ I learned that . . .

○ I still have questions about . . .

○ I feel confident about making a big decision because . . .

○ I feel hesitant about making a big decision because . . .

○ I will use what I have learned in the coming week by . . .

LISTENing for a Solution

Look for the facts. Identify details that might influence how the decision could be resolved. Figure out what the real situation is.

Imagine possibilities. Brainstorm all the options. Consider the consequences. Name the advantages and disadvantages of each option.

Seek insight beyond your own. Look for help from your family, your friends, and wise people you trust. If you are making a moral or ethical decision, find out what Jesus and the Church teach about the issue.

Turn inward. Examine your own feelings and insights from your experiences, motives, and values.

Expect God's help. Believe that God is present in your life, especially in your honest attempts to seek the truth.

Name your decision. Sometimes this means postponing the decision until you can do more thinking about it. Identify the reason for the delay.

LISTENing in the Quiet

Look for the facts.

- The decision I need to make is . . .
- The information I have is . . .
- My feelings about the situation are . . .

Imagine possibilities.

- Some options, along with the pluses and minuses of each, are . . .

Seek insight beyond your own.

- The people I want to talk to about this decision are . . .
- Church teaching and the Scriptures tell me that . . .

Turn inward.

- The values that are an important part of this decision are . . .
- The values that I'm not willing to compromise are . . .
- My inner voice tells me to . . .

Expect God's help.

- I want to pray about . . .
- I know God is with me in this because . . .

Name your decision.

- My decision is . . .
- My next step is . . .

Managing Life's Ups and Downs

Overview

No one is immune from stress. It is an ever-present part of our culture and our world. We can give young people a lifelong gift by giving them the tools to understand and deal with the stresses they face, that is, the changes, challenges, and occasional crises that are part of everyone's lives. This session helps young people see stress as unavoidable and potentially helpful. The opening activity shows them that a healthy amount of stress is necessary for creative productivity. An activity on identifying common stressors helps them to know that they are not alone in their struggles as teenagers in the twenty-first century. The closing reflection invites them to think about the internal and external resources that are available to them, gifts from their God, who is the eternal source of strength.

Outcomes

- The participants will identify the sources of stress in their lives and discover commonalities with other teens.
- The participants will examine life's struggles as moments of change, challenge, and crisis.

Background Reading

- Scriptural connections: Psalm 23 (The Lord is my shepherd.), Psalm 62 (Only in God is my soul at rest.), Matt. 11:28–30 (Come to me all who are weary.)
- *Catholic Youth Bible* article connections: "The Good Shepherd Looks After Us!" (Psalm 23), "The Big Picture" (Psalm 77), "A Spiritual Check-up" (2 Cor. 13:5–7)

AT A GLANCE

Study It

Core Session:
Handling the Stress of Life
(60 minutes)

- Focusing:
  Keeping Things Afloat
  (15 minutes)
- Discussion Exercise:
  Stressful Issues
  (30 minutes)
- Reflection:
  SOARing Through Life
  (15 minutes)

Pray It

- "Be Still, and Know
  That I Am God"
  (15 minutes)

Live It

- Fight or flight
- Just relax
- Scriptural struggles
- Stress outlets
- Where is God?
- The rest of the story
- Senior stress buster
- Managing the gift of time

Core Session:
Handling the Stress of Life (60 minutes)

Preparation
* Gather the following items:
  - ❑ inflated balloons of various sizes, a few more than the number of participants
  - ❑ copies of handout 5, "Stressful Issues," one for each participant
  - ❑ pens or pencils
  - ❑ newsprint
  - ❑ markers
  - ❑ masking tape
  - ❑ a candle (optional)
  - ❑ a recording of reflective music and the appropriate equipment (optional)
  - ❑ copies of handout 6, "SOARing Through Life," one for each participant (optional)
* Recruit someone to be an observer for the focusing activity, to count the number of times a balloon hits the ground (optional).

Focusing: Keeping Things Afloat (15 minutes)

   1. Display the balloons you inflated before the session, and explain that you will be tossing them into the middle of the group one by one. The group's task is to keep all the balloons in the air and not let any of them hit the ground. If you recruited an observer, explain that he or she will count the number of times balloons hit the ground.

   Ask everyone to keep track of three things:
* When is the game boring?
* When does the game get busy enough to be interesting?
* At what point does it become too much?

   2. Toss one or two balloons into the middle of the group. Keep tossing more in at regular intervals until you exhaust your supply. Make sure the game reaches a chaotic level. End the game when the participants have a difficult time keeping the balloons off the floor.

   3. Lead a discussion of the following questions:
* When was the game boring?

Try This

* Add new rules to the activity as you go along, such as the following ones:
  - ◇ Participants should play with their right hands behind their backs.
  - ◇ Girls (or boys) cannot touch the balloons. They should, however, stay in the group.
  - ◇ Participants cannot use their hands at all.
* You may want to insert a coin in some of the balloons to make the activity more interesting. The weight of the coin will make the balloons fly in unpredictable directions.

- When did the game get busy enough to be interesting? That is, when did you feel the most comfortable, energized, and successful?
- At what point did it become too much to handle? How did you react? How did the other group members react?

4. The beginning of the balloon activity will probably be evaluated as low energy and boring. The end of the game may have been frustrating and unsuccessful for the teens. The most energizing and productive part of the activity will probably be somewhere in the middle. Use the participants' comments, and make the following points in your own words:

- Stress is a normal and natural part of life. Too little stress causes people to become bored, complacent, and unmotivated. Too much stress is unhealthy.
- The best mixture of performance, interest, and energy came not at the beginning of our game, when the stress level was low, but rather in the middle, when the stress level was moderate.
- A certain amount of stress is not only helpful but also necessary for effective performance. Healthy stress keeps us alert and energized.
- The optimum stress level is different for each person, and depends on several variables, including physical, chemical, and emotional factors.

Discussion: Stressful Issues (30 minutes)

1. Divide the young people into small groups of four or five people. Distribute a copy of handout 5, "Stressful Issues," to each young person, and a sheet of newsprint and a marker to each small group. Explain that the small groups are to develop from the list on handout 5 a ranking of the top five most stressful issues facing young people today, then record it on their newsprint. The ranking should reflect what affects most of the young people the participants know.

2. Invite each group to share its ranking with everyone. Post the rankings and compare them.

3. Present the following information in your own words:

- Most stressful situations fall into one of three categories: challenges, changes, and crises. In many of those situations, we have no control over the events that are taking place. However, we usually have some control over our responses to those events.
- *Challenges* include things like peer pressure, dating, exams, competition, and confrontations with others. Not all challenges produce negative stress. Many are positive, and help us to be our best selves.
- *Changes* can be physical, emotional, spiritual, intellectual, or social. Experiences that fall into this category include going through puberty, falling in love, and developing a deeper understanding of God. Some

VARIATION:
Large Group

Divide the participants into two groups. You might add an element of competition, such as comparing which group lets the fewest balloons hit the floor.

Try This

- ◆ In step 1, have the young people complete handout 5, "Stressful Issues," individually before the small-group ranking exercise. They are likely to find many similarities to the small-group rankings, affirming that their feelings are not unusual.
- ◆ After all the lists of ranked issues are posted in step 2, distribute three adhesive dots to each person. Have everyone place their dots next to the issues they think are the biggest challenges for teens. Create a group composite list of the top five issues.

changes are circumstantial. Those include moving to a new school, having a sibling go away to college, or getting a driver's license.

- *Crises* are sudden, unexpected, or serious turning points in life. They include a death, parents divorcing, a major fight with a friend, a serious illness in the family, and winning a lottery. Crisis times are the ones for which we are least prepared. For that reason they are the most stressful and difficult times, even if they are exciting events.

- Understanding the classification of a stressful situation can help us prepare to deal with it by making decisions and taking actions that will optimize our opportunities for growth.

4. Review some of the ranked issues, and have the group identify them as challenges, changes, or crises.

Assign each small group one of the issues most commonly ranked in the top five, and give each group a sheet of newsprint. Reiterate that preparation is one of the keys to minimizing stress. Explain that the groups are to brainstorm ways to prepare to deal with their issues. For example, if the issue is expectations or pressure from other people, they might list the following steps:

- Increase communications skills so that I can discuss the situation confidently without conflict.
- Develop better time management skills so that I can make the most efficient use of my time.
- Find a trusted adult to help me sort out priorities and values.

Invite each group to share its brainstormed list of preparation strategies.

(This activity is adapted from Marilyn Kielbasa and Michael Theisen, *Taking Charge,* pp. 31–35.)

Reflection: SOARing Through Life (15 minutes)

1. Explain that human beings have an innate ability to make it through stressful situations, whether they are times of change, challenge, or crisis. To triumph in tough times, a person must carefully assess a situation and be willing to reach out.

Invite the teens to assume a comfortable position and quiet themselves inside and out. You may want to light a candle and play reflective music to set a meditative atmosphere.

Announce that you will lead them in a reflection on the SOAR model of dealing with stressful situations. Explain that *SOAR* is an acronym that stands for "strengths, opportunities, assistance, and roadblocks." Read the following reflection, pausing after each question:

- Think about a particular struggle in your life that is causing you stress. It may be a moment of change, challenge, or crisis. What is the struggle that you carry in your heart at this moment?

VARIATION:
Gender Groups

◆ Divide the teens into gender groups. Tell the young people to list from handout 5 the five most stressful issues that people of their gender face. Discuss the similarities and differences.

◆ Eliminate handout 5. Have each gender group brainstorm its own list of the most stressful issues for teens of its gender.

- The *S* in *SOAR* stands for "strength." You have strengths you can rely on to get you through anything. They may be your faith in God, your optimism, your perseverance, and any number of other factors. Those strengths are gifts from God. What are the strengths you will draw on to get you through?

- The *O* stands for "opportunities" that may help you overcome obstacles. Some examples are being on a sports team, which teaches you to overcome adversity in a positive way; ending a relationship that was heading in the wrong direction; and getting a part-time job that may help you define your career path. What opportunities has God placed in your life?

- The *A* stands for "assistance." Assistance is most clearly seen through the people in your life who are willing to walk with you through stressful times as well as good times. A source of assistance can be a parent, an older relative, a counselor, a youth minister, or another caring adult. Assistance may also come from an organization like a community center. Who and what are the sources of assistance in your life?

- The *R* in *SOAR* stands for "roadblocks." It may seem odd to name roadblocks as something that helps us through a problem, because roadblocks often create problems. But if you never encountered adversity, you would never need to look for and find the personal support that is within and around you. Roadblocks can be gifts, though it may be difficult to see them as such. What roadblocks stand in your way? How might those roadblocks be gifts in disguise?

2. Encourage the teens to think about SOARing whenever they are faced with a difficult situation. Remind them that strengths, opportunities, sources of assistance, and roadblocks are God's gifts to us as we journey through life. Close by reading Isa. 43:1–3, ending after the first two lines of verse 3.

(This activity is adapted from Marilyn Kielbasa and Michael Theisen, *Taking Charge*, pp. 49–50.)

Pray*It*

"Be Still, and Know That I Am God" (15 minutes)

Preparation

- You will need at least three sources of noise, such as a CD player and a recording of music or speech, a radio, a television, a loud appliance, or someone playing a musical instrument.
- Recruit someone to read Ps. 46:1–10.

TryThis

In step 1, distribute handout 6, "SOARing Through Life." Have the young people fill in the answers to the sentence starters after you explain each point of the reflection process. This option works well if extra time is available.

Spirit & Song
connections

- ◆ "Fly Like a Bird," by Ken Canedo
- ◆ "God's Eye Is on the Sparrow," by Bob Hurd
- ◆ "On Eagle's Wings," by Michael Joncas

- Recruit five readers, and give each one a segment of resource 3, "'Be Still, and Know That I Am God.'"
- Set up a prayer space with a candle and a *Catholic Youth Bible* or other Bible.

1. Gather the teens around the prayer space and invite them to be silent inside and out. After a few seconds, ask the reader to proclaim Ps. 46:1–10 in a normal tone of voice, repeating the line "Be still, and know that I am God" three times. As the reader begins, turn on the various sources of sound to a volume that is high enough so that the resulting cacophony will drown out the reader and be mildly annoying for the participants.

After the reading, shut everything off so that the room is silent. Allow the silence to linger for a few seconds.

2. Ask the young people what the last line of the reading was. Because of the noise, they probably did not hear it. Explain that the reader was proclaiming Ps. 46:1–10, which ended with, "Be still, and know that I am God."

Encourage them to discuss the connection between what they just experienced and coping with the stresses and struggles of life.

3. Invite the people who have segments of resource 3 to read their prayers in turn. Ask the participants to respond to each prayer with the verse, "Be still, and know that I am God."

4. Close with a spontaneous prayer on coping with life's struggles, or by reading Ps. 46:1–3,10.

Options and Actions

- **Fight or flight.** Lead a discussion of the ways people react to stress, sometimes known as the fight-or-flight response:
  - They confront and deal with their struggles and the stress those struggles produce (fight).
  - They run away from their struggles and avoid dealing with those struggles (flight).

  Present stressful scenarios, and ask the teens to discuss what each reaction might look like.
- **Just relax.** Lead the teens through relaxation exercises that progress through muscle groups, and teach the young people to do those exercises

Familyconnections

- ◆ Communicate information to parents on helping teens deal with the stresses in their lives. Include the results of the "Stressful Issues" exercise, suggestions for helping teens manage their time more efficiently, and ideas for discussing the issue of stress with teens.
- ◆ Suggest that parents discuss with their teens the stressful issues they faced as teens and how

on their own. Offer opportunities for guided meditation, which is a combination of relaxation and prayer. The series *A Quiet Place Apart* is a wonderful resource for guided meditations on a variety of topics, and the script for one of those meditations, "Soothing the Stress," is included on a handout on this manual's CD-ROM. Check out the twelve titles in the series at the Saint Mary's Press Web site, *www.smp.org.*

- **Scriptural struggles.** Explore the following scriptural passages, and decide if the main character in each story (noted in parentheses) is experiencing a moment of change, challenge, or crisis:
  - Jer. 1:4–10 (Jeremiah)
  - Matt. 4:1–11 (Jesus)
  - Mark 10:17–22 (the rich man)
  - Luke 1:26–38 (Mary)
  - John 2:1–11 (Jesus)
  - John 8:2–11 (a woman)
  - Rom. 7:15–25 (Paul)

- **Stress outlets.** Brainstorm ways that young people deal with stress in their lives. For example, some handle stress in a healthy way by doing some physical activity or by playing an instrument. Others have unhealthy ways of dealing with it, such as resorting to alcohol to help them relax or reacting violently when difficulties arise.

- **Where is God?** Write the letters GODISNOWHERE on a flip chart. Ask the young people what they see. Chances are good that someone will see "God is nowhere" before anyone sees "God is now here." Write each phrase at the head of a separate column on a flip chart. Ask the teens to call out the feelings one would associate with each phrase. Discuss how a simple shift of one letter alters the entire meaning. Make the connection with seeing God as a source of strength among life's difficulties.

- **The rest of the story.** Paul Harvey, a legendary radio personality, featured stories of people who triumphed over difficulties. Those timeless stories are collected in a book called *Paul Harvey's the Rest of the Story* (New York: Bantam Books, reissued ed. 1984.) Share some of the stories with the teens, inviting them to predict the outcomes before telling them how each person's story ends. Have the teens write an autobiographical piece in the same format.

- **Senior stress buster.** Invite high school seniors to an evening or a day devoted to looking at the particular changes and challenges associated with leaving high school. Provide opportunities for sharing, relaxation, meditation, prayer, goal setting, and planning for the next steps.

- **Managing the gift of time.** Conduct a session on the skills of effective time-management. Invite busy teens who seem to manage their time well to share their secrets. Discuss setting priorities and making realistic commitments. Explore time-management tools offered by various calendar and planning programs.

they handled the situations. Those issues would also make for an interesting conversation in an intergenerational group that includes senior citizens.

JournalACTIVITIES

- List all the things that are stressors in your life right now. Divide them into the categories of change, challenge, and crisis. What can you do to show that you deal with each situation in a helpful and healthy way?
- Set aside one page in your journal for strengths, one for opportunities, one for assistance, and one for roadblocks. Keep a running list of the gifts God places in your life to help you cope.

Stressful Issues

Rank the following items from **1** to **25,** with **1** being the most stressful to teens you know, and **25** being the least stressful.

_____ changing schools

_____ conflicts with parents

_____ decisions about life after high school

_____ the breakup of a relationship

_____ physical appearance

_____ being liked by others

_____ a schedule that is too busy

_____ grades or teachers

_____ physical development

_____ the separation or divorce of parents

_____ blending with another family because of remarriage

_____ using drugs or alcohol

_____ pressure to be more sexually active

_____ rejection or failure

_____ arguing between parents

_____ the death of someone close

_____ having enough money

_____ violence at school or at home

_____ dating

_____ expectations of other people

_____ conflicts with peers

_____ competition

_____ athletic ability

_____ other: _____

_____ other: _____

(This handout is adapted from Marilyn Kielbasa and Michael Theisen, _Taking Charge: Managing Life's Struggles_ [Winona, MN: Saint Mary's Press, 1996], page 42, copyright © 1996 by Saint Mary's Press, all rights reserved.)

SOARing Through Life

A situation I struggle with is . . .

Strengths are the gifts, talents, and abilities we possess.
My strengths are . . .

Opportunities are situations that allow us to grow and develop.
My opportunities are . . .

Assistance comes from people and places that are present to us and willing
to help when we need them. My sources of assistance are . . .

Roadblocks are challenges that lead us to discover the internal and
external resources in our lives. My roadblocks are . . .

(This handout is adapted from Marilyn Kielbasa and Michael Theisen, *Taking Charge: Managing Life's Struggles* [Winona, MN: Saint Mary's Press, 1996], page 64, copyright © 1996 by Saint Mary's Press, all rights reserved.)

"Be Still, and Know That I Am God"

Reader 1: "God is our refuge and our strength, present to us in all our joys and struggles, in our changes, challenges, and crises. We rely on God's constant presence and care (adapted from Psalm 46:1)."

Reader 2: "We will not fear, though the earth and everything in it is constantly changing. We will not lose hope, though sometimes it seems like things are falling apart (adapted from Psalm 46:2–3)."

Reader 3: "In every place we are, there is God. God is with us when we wake up and when we close our eyes. God knows every thought, feeling, word, and action. God knows every fiber of our being (adapted from Psalm 46:4–7)."

Reader 4: "Behold all that God has done. Look at all that God has given us. God takes care of all our needs. God gives us people to love and people who love us. God is the source of all that is good (adapted from Psalm 46:8–9)."

Reader 5: "Be still, and know that God is kind and good, loving and generous. Be still, and know that God is powerful and mighty, loyal and just. Be still, and know that God is (adapted from Psalm 46:10)."

8 Handling Anger, Managing Conflict

Overview

Anger is a basic human emotion, and conflict is the inevitable result when anger comes between people who are in relationship with each other. When people express anger in loud, hostile, or violent ways—or do not express it at all—relationships suffer. This session gives the young people the opportunity to explore their attitudes toward anger through a voting activity. A survey on handling conflict helps them discover if their typical conflict-management style is helpful in solving the problems in their relationships. Finally, a discussion teaches them a process for evaluating and addressing conflicts in a positive and appropriate way.

Outcomes

◆ The participants will identify some ways they deal with anger and conflict.

◆ The participants will learn a process for dealing with conflict in a positive way.

Background Reading

◆ Scriptural connections: Matt. 18:21–22 (a challenge to forgive), John 2:13–17 (the cleansing of the Temple), John 15:12–13 (Jesus' command to love one another)

◆ *Catholic Youth Bible* article connections: "Facing Life's Battles" (Deut. 20:1), "Hotheads" (Prov. 22:24–25), "Righteous Anger" (John 2:13–17)

AT A GLANCE

Study It

Core Session:
Anger, Conflict, and PEACE
(60 minutes)

◆ Focusing:
Thoughts on Anger and Conflict
(15 minutes)

◆ Survey and Presentation:
Handling Conflict
(20 minutes)

◆ Discussion:
The PEACE Process
(25 minutes)

Pray It

◆ Living in Peace
(15 minutes)

Live It

◆ Conflict graffiti
◆ Scriptural values
◆ Angry expressions
◆ Conflict resolution
◆ Assertiveness training
◆ Great escapes

Core Session:
Anger, Conflict, and PEACE (60 minutes)

Preparation

- Gather the following items:
  - ❏ copies of handout 7, "How I Handle Conflict," one for each participant
  - ❏ pens or pencils
  - ❏ copies of handout 8, "Survey Score Sheet," one for each participant
  - ❏ newsprint and a marker
  - ❏ copies of handout 9, "The PEACE Process," one for each participant
- Write the following information on newsprint, with the letters *P-E-A-C-E* listed down the left side of the page:

  P: Problem and Purpose

  E: Empathy

  A: Accountability

  C: Choices

  E: Engage and Express

Focusing: Thoughts on Anger and Conflict (15 minutes)

1. Introduce the session by pointing out that anger is a common human emotion and that conflict is part of every relationship. Handling anger and managing conflict are important skills to learn if we are to become peaceful people, and if we want our relationships to thrive.

Explain that you will read several statements about anger and conflict, and that the teens should respond in one of three ways:

- I agree, symbolized by two thumbs up
- I disagree, symbolized by two thumbs down
- I'm not sure, symbolized by arms crossed over the chest

2. Read the following statements, allowing the participants time to respond after each one. Do not offer comments during the responses.

- Everyone feels angry sometimes.
- Jesus felt anger.
- Jesus was never in conflict with anyone.
- Expressing anger is a negative thing to do.

- It is okay to feel angry when someone hurts me.
- A Christian should never be in conflict with anyone.
- "Don't get mad, get even" is a good motto for dealing with anger.
- Expressing anger immediately is the best way to deal with it.
- Two people who experience many conflicts can never be good friends.
- If someone makes me angry and I blow up, it's their fault.
- Expressing anger can help build a better relationship.

3. Invite the young people to comment or ask questions. Then make the following comments in your own words:

- Anger is a normal reaction to frustration and hurt. Like any other emotion, it is neither good nor bad. It just exists. Feelings of anger may be directed at another person, a group of people, ourselves, and even God.
- Everyone experiences anger and the conflict that often results. Even Jesus expressed anger when he threw the merchants from the Temple. He found himself in conflict with many people.
- Emotions do not go away. If they are not expressed appropriately, they will be released in negative ways, such as through depression, withdrawal, anxiety, physical problems, or blowing up over trivial things.
- If we do not learn how to control our emotions, they will control us. We must choose how to react to and express our feelings. That choice is in our control.
- Christians experience anger and conflict in their relationships. However, instead of letting their anger hurt them or their relationships, they choose to deal with it in Christian ways—by being honest about it, expressing it without attacking others, and being willing to forgive.

Survey and Presentation: Handling Conflict (20 minutes)

1. Distribute handout 7, "How I Handle Conflict," and pens or pencils. Explain to the teens that they are going to test themselves to discover their preferred style for dealing with conflict. Tell them to read each situation and choose the best response. If no choice matches their reaction, they should pick the one that is closest to the way they would likely behave. If none of the first three choices comes close to their possible reaction, they may choose the fourth option, "none of the above."

2. Allow about 5 minutes for the teens to complete the survey; then distribute handout 8, "Survey Score Sheet." Explain that this sheet will help them identify their preferred style for dealing with anger and conflict. Tell them to enter a check mark on the line before the letter of their response to each question, emphasizing that the score sheet does not list the choices in alphabetical order.

VARIATION:
Gender Groups

Men and women, girls and boys handle anger differently. For boys, anger, if unchecked, can often manifest itself as violence and rage. For girls, the result is often depression (sometimes described as anger turned inward). Gather the young people in gender groups to discuss those realities, to look at the things that trigger anger, and to brainstorm positive ways for each gender to manage its anger.

When they finish recording their answers, they should tally the number of check marks in each column to discover which coping technique they prefer to use when they are in conflict.

3. Convey the following information in your own words:

- There are different ways of coping with anger. Some are productive and resolve conflicts. Others are often not productive. Three strategies that are not productive are fighting, retreating, and ignoring:

  ◦ *Fighting* includes both verbal hostility (arguing, being sarcastic, putting people down, and name-calling) and physical hostility. The result of fighting is often hurt, resentment, bitterness, and increased anger.

  ◦ *Retreating* includes running away from the situation and avoiding dealing with anger directly. Examples of retreating include trying to get an authority to take care of a problem, resigning from a group, and giving someone the silent treatment. The outcome of retreating is that the conflict is not resolved, no one accepts responsibility for their contributions to the conflict, and no one has an opportunity to change and grow.

  ◦ *Ignoring* includes refusing to notice feelings of anger, telling oneself that one really does not care, and trying to avoid one's feelings by excusing the other person. Possible outcomes of ignoring anger are feelings of depression and a sense of loss of control of one's life.

Draw the teens' attention to the survey score sheet. Explain that the letters at the tops of the columns stand for *fighting, retreating, ignoring,* and *none of the above.* Ask them to see if they have chosen one of the three ineffective strategies more often than another.

If anyone checked choice *d,* "none of the above," most often, suggest that they probably would have dealt with most of the problems using a more productive approach than the ones described in *a, b,* and *c.*

Conclude the activity by making the following points:

- God created each of us with a unique personality that influences how we deal with conflict. How we handle our feelings of anger can change from one situation to another.

- In difficult cases, verbal fighting, running, or ignoring may be the only options we have, but in most cases, those three strategies are not the best ways to solve conflict. As peacemakers, we are called to develop skills in the most productive ways of dealing with conflict.

Discussion: The PEACE Process (25 minutes)

1. Acknowledge that everyone has moments when relationships are strained. Point out that those moments must be dealt with so that relationships can stay healthy. Explain to the participants that they are going to learn a process that can help them resolve conflicts in their relationships.

Display the information you wrote on newsprint before the session. Distribute copies of handout 9, "The PEACE Process." Spend 5 to 10 minutes reviewing the elements of the process.

2. Divide the participants into small groups. Assign each group one situation from handout 7, "How I Handle Conflict." Instruct the groups to use the PEACE process to devise an effective way to deal with the conflict.

Allow about 5 minutes for the groups to complete their work, then invite them to share the results with everyone.

3. Make the following points in your own words:
- Any conflict requires that we keep the lines of communication open. If we do not talk with those with whom we disagree, we have little chance of solving the problem. We must take the energy we use to be angry and put it into finding new ways to solve problems and heal troubled relationships.
- If we acknowledge that we have a right to our feelings and that our anger is justified, we can use the PEACE process to resolve a conflict in a relationship without destroying it. Everyone who is involved has the potential for growth.
- Growth includes recognizing failings, taking responsibility for them, asserting ourselves so that our basic emotional needs are met, and working toward a positive outcome. If we fail to do those things, we are in danger of repeating behaviors that contributed to the destruction of the relationship.
- Some conflicts in relationships cannot be resolved, such as when values collide or when one person is not open to accepting responsibility for her or his part in the conflict. If we have sincerely tried to resolve a conflict and failed, we must forgive the other person and move on.

Close by reading Rom. 12:16–21, Saint Paul's response to those who want to get even or desire revenge.

(This session is adapted from Gail Daniels Hassett, *Becoming a Peacemaker,* pp. 29–37.)

Pray It

Living in Peace (15 minutes)

Preparation
- Gather the following items:
  - ❏ a candle and matches
  - ❏ a *Catholic Youth Bible* or other Bible

TryThis
- ◆ Instead of using the situations from handout 9 for the application of the PEACE process, use a real situation in the school or in the community that does not directly involve the participants.
- ◆ As an alternative to the small-group work or in addition to it, give the young people some reflection time to apply the PEACE process to a conflict situation in their own life.

❑ a recording of reflective music and the appropriate equipment (optional)
- Set up a prayer space with a candle and a Bible.
- Recruit two readers, and assign one of the following passages to each:
  ○ Rom. 12:16–18
  ○ Rom. 12:19–21

1. Gather the group around the prayer space. Invite the young people to quiet themselves. You may want to play reflective music if it is available.

After a moment of quiet, ask the young people to remember a recent time when they were in conflict with someone. Then, using the following questions, guide the young people through a reflection on their experience. Allow a moment of silence after each question.
- What feelings did you experience about yourself? about the other person?
- What did you want to do?
- What did you do?
- What would you change about the experience, if you could?

2. Explain that Saint Paul recognized how easy it is to want to get even or get revenge. He encouraged us to respond as Christians. Invite the first reader to proclaim Rom. 12:16–18.

3. Tell the young people to think about what they must do to live in peace with the situation they recalled. Ask them to pray for the strength and courage to do what is necessary to heal the conflict, and the patience to wait for the healing to happen.

After a few minutes, invite the second reader to proclaim Rom. 12:19–21. Close by inviting the teens to make a firm commitment to becoming peacemakers in their relationships.

Options and Actions

- **Conflict graffiti.** Post three sheets of newsprint. Write one of the following headings on each sheet:
  ○ My pet peeve is . . .
  ○ I get *so* angry when . . .
  ○ When I'm angry, I . . .
Invite the young people to complete each sentence starter by writing their thoughts under the appropriate heading.

Familyconnections

◆ Share the PEACE process with families. Suggest that they apply the steps to a current family conflict, discussing them as they go through them.

◆ After the conflict survey, consider having the teens create conflict scenarios

- **Scriptural values.** Divide the teens into small groups, and assign each group one of the following scriptural citations. Ask them to identify the important thing Jesus said or did in their passage and the peacemaking values reflected in the words or the act. Those values might include courage, compassion, standing up for a belief, forgiveness, and a commitment to peace.
  - Matt. 5:23–24
  - Matt. 5:43–44
  - Matt. 18:21–22
  - Matt. 21:12–13
  - Luke 10:30–36
  - Luke 22:24–26
  - John 8:3–11
  - John 15:12–13
- **Angry expressions.** Ask the teens to quickly name ways of expressing anger that they see used by people they know (without actually naming them), and list their responses as they do so. When the list is complete, ask them to identify the expressions as positive or negative and to explain what makes them so.
- **Conflict resolution.** Invite someone from the local community to facilitate a program on conflict resolution so that the teens can further develop their skills. Check with school districts, mental-health agencies, mediation services, and human resource departments in local businesses for names of people who can do that type of training.
- **Assertiveness training.** People can be aggressive, assertive, or passive. Of the three, assertiveness is the most positive approach to getting their needs met. Sponsor a session on assertiveness training, focusing on skills like using "I messages," negotiating, saying no and meaning it, and claiming personal power. Consult the resources listed in the "Conflict resolution" option for names of people who are trained to facilitate such a session.
- **Great escapes.** Brainstorm with the youth a list of positive outlets for anger. Keep the list in a visible place, or create easy-reference bookmarks for the young people to carry with them.

that typically occur in family life. Have them create responses that fit each of the categories. Use this new survey as the basis for a gathering of families with teens. Consider including a reconciliation service.

◆ Follow this session with the intergenerational session on parent-teen communication, in chapter 10.

Mediaconnections

Check out *www.textweek. com, www.teachwithmovies. org,* and *www.hollywood jesus.com* for lists of movies on the session theme. Check out the ratings, the commentary, and the connections to the theme, and decide what is appropriate for your group.

JournalACTIVITIES

◆ How have you dealt with anger in the past? Would you deal differently with it now? How so?

◆ What have you discovered about how you handle conflict?

◆ What can you do to make a difference in the way you deal with problems in your relationships?

How I Handle Conflict

Read each situation, and place a check mark next to the response that best reflects how you would react in that situation.

1. If someone kept saying something I strongly disagreed with, I would . . .
   _____ **a.** make a sarcastic comment
   _____ **b.** change the subject
   _____ **c.** say I was wrong even if I did not think I was, to keep the peace
   _____ **d.** none of the above

2. If a friend was angry with me and began to yell and argue, I would . . .
   _____ **a.** walk away and avoid the whole thing
   _____ **b.** decide my friend was having a bad day and his anger didn't have much to do with me
   _____ **c.** yell back
   _____ **d.** none of the above

3. If someone who was assigned to work on a school project with me did not do his or her fair share, and as a result I received a poor grade, I would . . .
   _____ **a.** tell the person how unfair and lazy he or she was
   _____ **b.** complain to the teacher
   _____ **c.** forget the whole thing
   _____ **d.** none of the above

4. If I found that someone was spreading rumors about me, I would . . .
   _____ **a.** confront the person and call him or her a liar
   _____ **b.** avoid the person and those who were listening to him or her
   _____ **c.** wonder what I did to make the person do that
   _____ **d.** none of the above

5. If I told a friend I failed my driver's test, and the friend made fun of me and told everyone about it, I would . . .
   _____ **a.** feel hurt but pretend it did not matter
   _____ **b.** feel hurt and blame myself for telling that friend in the first place
   _____ **c.** tease that friend about something at which I knew she or he had failed
   _____ **d.** none of the above

6. If money was missing from the place where I worked, and a coworker told the boss and other people that I might have taken it, I would . . .

_____ **a.** wait until after work and have a fight with the coworker

_____ **b.** complain to the boss about how insulted I was

_____ **c.** quit my job

_____ **d.** none of the above

7. If my parents told me on Wednesday that I had to stay home on Friday night to watch my younger siblings, and this would ruin my plans with my friends, I would . . .

_____ **a.** stay home, but let my parents know how mad I was by giving everyone the silent treatment

_____ **b.** refuse to do it and leave

_____ **c.** feel that I really should not be angry because my parents probably had a good reason

_____ **d.** none of the above

8. If I were having a difficult time with a class at school, and a classmate made fun of me, I would . . .

_____ **a.** pretend I was ill, and skip the class until I could get some help

_____ **b.** start calling the other person names

_____ **c.** ignore the other person

_____ **d.** none of the above

9. If I had been waiting in line to purchase something, and just as I got to the front of the line, the clerk turned to wait on an older person who had just walked up, I would . . .

_____ **a.** feel annoyed but do nothing

_____ **b.** make a sarcastic comment

_____ **c.** leave the item on the counter and walk away angry

_____ **d.** none of the above

10. If I had a friend who promised to come over and do homework with me but instead went to the movies with someone else, I would . . .

_____ **a.** be embarrassed about being stood up

_____ **b.** tell other friends what a jerk that person was

_____ **c.** avoid that person until he or she apologized to me

_____ **d.** none of the above

Survey Score Sheet

Place a check mark on the line before the choice you made for each situation. When you have finished recording your choices, tally the number of check marks in each column. **Note:** The choices are *not* listed in alphabetical order.

	F	**R**	**I**	**N**
1.	_____ a	_____ c	_____ b	_____ d
2.	_____ c	_____ a	_____ b	_____ d
3.	_____ a	_____ b	_____ c	_____ d
4.	_____ a	_____ c	_____ b	_____ d
5.	_____ c	_____ b	_____ a	_____ d
6.	_____ a	_____ b	_____ c	_____ d
7.	_____ a	_____ b	_____ c	_____ d
8.	_____ b	_____ a	_____ c	_____ d
9.	_____ b	_____ a	_____ c	_____ d
10.	_____ b	_____ c	_____ a	_____ d
Totals	☐	☐	☐	☐

The PEACE Process

P: Problem and Purpose
- Ask yourself, "What is the problem, and is it important enough to make an issue of it?"
- Ask yourself, "What do I hope to accomplish by telling the other person how I feel?"

E: Empathy
- Listen with an open mind to what the other person is saying, and try to put yourself in the other person's shoes.
- Respect the other person's feelings.

A: Accountability
- Take responsibility for any contribution you may have made to the conflict.
- Reflect on the reasons why you reacted the way you did.

C: Choices
- Think about all the possible ways to solve this problem.
- Ask yourself: "What solutions are best for this relationship? What solutions respect my need to be heard, respected, and valued?"

E: Engage and Express
- Calmly express how you feel. Tell the person what he or she did and explain why you feel the way you do.
- State your position without attacking the other person.
- Express your willingness to come to a positive solution.

Dealing with Life's Changes

Overview

As much as we would like to think otherwise, change is constant. Most of the changes we experience—even good ones—result in losses. Young people share in universal experiences of change and the resulting loss, such as death and changes in relationships. They also have experiences of change that are unique to their age, such as graduations, team tryouts, and puberty. Helping teens identify and deal with the positive and negative changes and resulting losses in their lives teaches them valuable coping skills for the changes they have yet to face.

Outcomes

- ◆ The participants will understand the nature of change—its opportunities and its consequences.
- ◆ The participants will explore the loss that accompanies change as a common and shared experience among all human beings.
- ◆ The participants will explore ways to cope with and grow through change and loss.

Background Reading

- ◆ Scriptural connections: Ps. 22:1–5 (a prayer for deliverance), Lam. 3:31–33 (God's compassion for those who grieve), John 14:18–20,27 (Jesus' words of peace)
- ◆ *Catholic Youth Bible* article connections: "Growing Through Loss" (Lamentations, chap. 5), "Thumbs Up!" (Zech. 8:9–17)

Core Session:
Life's Changes, Life's Losses
(60 minutes)

Preparation

- Gather the following items:
  - ❑ copies of handout 10, "The Category Is . . . ," one for each small group
  - ❑ pens or pencils
  - ❑ a flip chart and a marker
  - ❑ a recording of reflective music and the appropriate equipment (optional)
  - ❑ copies of handout 11, "Changes and Losses in My Life," one for each participant (optional)
  - ❑ 3-by-3-inch pieces of paper, about three for each participant
  - ❑ rolls of cellophane tape, one for each small group
  - ❑ 5-foot lengths of ribbon or string, one for each small group
- Write the following quote on a flip chart: "Nothing endures but change" (Heraclitus, c. 540–c. 480 B.C.).
- List the following items on another page of the flip chart:
  - ○ changing schools
  - ○ a sudden illness
  - ○ graduation
  - ○ getting cut from a team
  - ○ the separation of parents
  - ○ getting a part-time job
- Make a sign that says, "Loss Lifelines," and post it on an easel or a blank wall.

Focusing: The Category Is . . .
(15 minutes)

1. Divide the young people into teams of five or six. Give each team a copy of handout 10, "The Category Is . . . ," and a pen or a pencil. Explain that the words in each group on the handout have something in common. The task is to read the words and phrases in each group and identify the category that unites all the words. For example, *center, defense, travel, dribble, foul,* and *hoop* are all terms used in the game of basketball.

TryThis

- ◆ To save time, keep everyone together, eliminate handout 10, and read or post the items from each group of words. Ask the entire group to work together to name the category for each group.

◆ Do this exercise in the format of the game show *$25,000 Pyramid.* Have one person read the items to another, and have the second person guess the category. Set a time limit of 30 seconds. Award small prizes for the pair that finishes in the least amount of time. You may want to add items to the categories and add other categories to provide enough variety.

2. Allow no more than 5 minutes for the small groups to work; then compare their answers. For your information, the categories are named here:
- *Group 1:* cocurricular activities
- *Group 2:* things teenagers might do on a weekend
- *Group 3:* ways to express emotion
- *Group 4:* unhealthy ways of dealing with difficulties
- *Group 5:* changes in life that result in loss

The teens may have a difficult time naming the last category as life's changes. They may recognize the items as challenges, but may not make the connection with changes and the subsequent losses they produce. Note that loss results even from positive events, like graduation or getting a job.

Discussion: Change and the Continuum of Loss (20 minutes)

1. Display the quote that you wrote on a flip chart before the session. Lead a discussion of the following questions:
- What are some positive examples that illustrate the quote? What are some difficult ones?
- What is the connection between change and loss?

2. Make the following points in your own words:
- As ironic as it seems, the only thing that never changes is change. God is the only exception to that rule. The world around us and within us constantly changes. Our bodies, even when they are at rest, engage in a flurry of activity as blood pumps, cells divide, hair grows, and air moves in and out of the lungs.
- Life is constantly changing as well. Relationships get stronger; some break apart. People learn more about themselves and the world every day. The details of life get rearranged as people move, join and quit groups, and pursue new interests.
- Changes may be personal, such as starting a new relationship or moving. They may be communal, such as war or the arrival of a new pastor at your church. Some changes may be welcome ones, like the additional spending money from a new part-time job. Other changes are painful ones, such as the separation of parents.
- Every change brings loss, even if the change is a good one. Without change we would not be able to grow as human beings or as a society. A deep sense of loss comes along with a dramatic change, such as the death of someone close to us. Other changes may be less significant, but may still produce a real sense of loss for those who experience them.
- The message of Jesus was about change—changing the heart of society and of individuals within it to bring about God's Reign.

3. Display the flip chart page listing the items from group 5 of handout 10. Ask the young people to suggest other losses people experience, and add them to the newsprint. Discuss the nature of the loss in some of the less obvious circumstances. Some examples follow:

- Getting cut from a sports team might mean the loss of a dream for someone—the dream of an athletic scholarship or playing for a prestigious college.
- Graduation is a welcome change for most people, but it usually means leaving friends behind and the loss of a familiar routine and an established track record.
- Poor health might mean a loss of independence, an inability to participate in enjoyable activities, and a heightened sense of mortality.
- Getting a part-time job means that a person has more money and may learn valuable skills. However, it might also mean less time for friends, family, or activities like sports or reading for pleasure.

4. Explain that every loss in a person's life can be placed on a continuum that represents the degree of intensity. For example, if a pet dies, one person might experience only a temporary sadness if that person was not particularly attached to the pet. In that case the sense of loss would be low intensity. Another person might experience a high sense of loss if the pet had been with the family for a long time and the person and the pet were constant companions during childhood.

Invite the young peoples' comments and observations. Close by making the following comments:

- We do not know how a loss will impact us until we experience it. One person's loss is like no one else's. Each person reacts to loss differently, handles it differently, and recovers from it differently.
- No matter how big or small the loss may be, we grieve. That is true whether the change that precipitated the loss is positive or negative. Grieving is a process that can be thought of as a pathway. Every person walks the path differently. We may go back and forth along the path, and we may get stuck somewhere.
- In situations where the loss is deep and painful, we may go through feelings of denial, anger, confusion, despair, powerlessness, fear, aloneness, depression, longing, and peace. When the loss is not major, we may not experience all those feelings.
- To be healthy we must allow ourselves to grieve our losses—even those that result from good changes. We must encourage others to grieve their losses, and support them in the process. We must look to God for courage and strength to stay on the path to wholeness.

TryThis

If your group is made up of juniors and seniors, focus part of the discussion on losses they will experience in the near future, including leaving the familiarity of high school, leaving friends, moving away, and so forth. Such a discussion will help them prepare for the inevitable transition.

TryThis

Distribute copies of handout 11, "Changes and Losses in My Life," or write the hand-out's sentence starters on a flip chart. Encourage the young people to spend about 10 minutes writing their reflections.

Reflection: Changes and Losses in My Life (5 minutes)

Invite the young people to assume a comfortable position and to be silent inside and out. Tell them that you will read several sentence starters, each followed by a short pause so they can think about their answers. You may want to play reflective music to enhance the atmosphere.

When they are ready, read the following sentence starters, pausing for about 30 seconds after each one:

- A significant change I recently experienced is . . .
- Because of that change, I lost . . .
- From that change, I learned . . .
- I still have questions about . . .
- Something positive that came out of the change is . . .
- The things that got me through the difficult times were . . .

Discussion: Loss Lifelines (20 minutes)

1. Make the following comments in your own words:

- All of nature experiences the same cycle of constant change and renewal. When we experience loss resulting from such a cycle, we share the rhythm of the universe. From life comes death comes life. It is the same cycle that Christians call the Paschal mystery, that is, the Passion, death, and Resurrection of Jesus Christ.
- Many resources exist to help us cope with the losses and changes in our lives. Coping might be as simple as talking to a caring friend or finding a physical outlet. It might be more complex if the loss is deep and enduring.
- We learn how to handle big losses by remembering how we coped with the less significant ones. Remembering how we made it through difficult situations in the past is the key to surviving them in the future.

2. Ask the teens to recall their answers to the last sentence starter, "The things that got me through the difficult times were . . ." Comment that these were their loss lifelines—people, activities, thoughts, and attitudes that got them through difficult times. Some loss lifelines that people rely on include these:

- a caring peer or adult who listened
- good memories
- a deep faith in God
- an awareness that one has survived losses before and will do so again
- remembering ways one dealt with earlier losses

Tell the young people to gather in the same small groups they were in at the beginning of the session. Give each small group a stack of small pieces of paper, a roll of cellophane tape, and a length of ribbon or string. Explain that each group is to create a composite lifeline by writing individual suggestions on a separate piece of paper and attaching the papers to the string or ribbon. Invite the participants to begin by talking about items they named during the reflection period, and note that they are not limited to those items. Allow about 10 minutes for the groups to do their work.

3. Invite someone from each group to read the lifelines; then attach the group's ribbon or string under the "Loss Lifelines" sign you posted before the session began.

Call the young people's attention to the number and variety of lifelines, emphasizing that no one has to navigate life's challenges alone. God orchestrates many changes in life, and God knows the pain we sometimes feel because of them. To help us cope, God gives us the gifts of faith, hope, and one another.

Conclude by reading Psalm 121.

Losses and Learnings (20 minutes)

Preparation
- Gather the following items
  - ❑ a pillar candle and matches
  - ❑ a *Catholic Youth Bible* or other Bible
  - ❑ a cross or a crucifix
  - ❑ the lifelines from the previous activity, "Loss Lifelines"
  - ❑ votive candles, one for each participant
  - ❑ one or more copies of resource 5, "Words of Comfort"
  - ❑ a basket
  - ❑ a taper candle
- Set up a prayer table with a pillar candle, a Bible, and a cross or a crucifix. Attach the lifelines so that they stream from the table. The table should be large enough to accommodate votive candles for everyone.
- Cut apart one or more copies of resource 5 as scored, and place the pieces in a basket. You will need one quote for every teen.

1. Gather the young people around the prayer table, and give each person an unlit votive candle. Invite them to recall the reflection time during the previous activity. In particular ask them to think about these two sentence starters:

Spirit & Song connections
- ◆ "Lord of All Hopefulness," by Timothy R. Smith
- ◆ "Revive Us, O God," by Jesse Manibusan

Familyconnections

◆ Family life is always changing—children grow, parents get new jobs and pursue new interests, families experience birth, illness, and death. Ask the youth to reflect on a change in their families over the last year. Use the reflection questions from the session, but apply them to that change. Ask the youth to reflect on these questions: How can I be a loss lifeline in my family as we experience change? Who can I turn to as a lifeline in my family?

◆ Invite the youth to discuss change and loss with one or both of their parents. The discussion might focus on the following questions:

◇ What change was important in your life?

◇ What feelings do you associate with that change?

◇ What learning or growth do you connect with that change?

• A significant change I recently experienced is . . .

• From that change I learned . . .

You may need to give examples like the following ones:

• My best friend moved last summer. I learned that we are still very much part of each other's lives because we communicate regularly. And I've also found new friends.

• I didn't make the team this year. That was hard. But I learned that my parents are really caring people. I also learned that there's more to life than basketball.

Note that some changes are too fresh for us to realize the lessons they hold. In those cases, the teens may just want to name the situations and lift them to God in silent prayer.

2. Use the following process for the prayer ritual:

• Each person in turn brings her or his candle to the table and uses the taper candle to light it from the pillar candle.

• If they wish to do so, the teens can briefly share their experience and what they learned from it. Assure them that no one has to share their thoughts if they are uncomfortable doing so.

• Each person should take a scriptural quote from the basket and read it to the group. They should leave their candle on the table, but take the quote with them.

Invite the teens to come forward as they are ready to do so. Close by reading Ps. 121:5–8.

Options and Actions

• **Guided meditation.** *Guided Meditations for Ordinary Time,* part of the series A Quiet Place Apart, by Jane E. Ayer, includes a meditation on loss. It is available through Saint Mary's Press. Call 800-533-8095, or visit the Web site, *www.smp.org.*

• **Lifeline lists.** Compile the lifelines from the "Loss Lifelines" activity into a list. Add others, including community resources, grief counseling services, support groups, and so forth. Include appropriate scriptural quotes. Give each young person a copy of the lifelines for his or her own reference.

• **Tough times survival kit.** Provide blank books, and have each person create, over a period of time, her or his own resource for dealing with life's difficulties. The kit might include the following items:

- an "I Survived" section, where the young person can write about tough situations and how he or she got through them
- inspirational quotes, pictures, song lyrics, and poetry
- scriptural verses that speak of hope
- stories of people who have had similar experiences
- lifeline lists, that is, names of people and groups to reach out to in tough times
- a section for writing prayers and other thoughts
- a list of positive coping strategies

- **Grief work.** Invite someone from the community for a discussion of the stages of grief, coping strategies, and grief-work skills. The person should be someone who is involved in hospice, bereavement ministry, or another area of service to people who struggle with loss.

- **Loss in the Scriptures.** Have the young people read and discuss the following passages from the perspective of change, loss, and coping. If you have *Catholic Youth Bibles* available, use the corresponding articles as starting points.
  - 2 Sam. 18:33—19:8 (King David mourns the death of his son.)
  - Job 2:11–13 (Job's friends stick by him.)
  - John 11:1–37 (Jesus' friend Lazarus dies.)
  - Acts 20:36–38 (Paul says good-bye to his friends at Ephesus.)

- **Still wondering.** As part of a reflection and discussion exercise, ask the young people to think of their least answerable questions about loss. Just posing the questions and being willing to struggle with them is already part of the answer. Questions like those require not so much answers of the mind but answers from the heart (adapted from Nancy Marrocco, *Death, Grief, and Christian Hope,* p. 24).

- **Hope markers.** Have the young people create bookmarks with inspirational quotes and scriptural verses written on them. For example, one bookmark would include the quote "Nothing endures but change" on one side, and the scriptural quote "I am with you always" (Matt. 28:20) on the other side. The bookmarks could be made available to people in the parish who are struggling with difficult changes. Provide quote books and a variety of art materials for this task.

- **Praying our good-byes.** The book *Praying Our Goodbyes,* by Joyce Rupp (Notre Dame, IN: Ave Maria Press, 1989), is a valuable resource for dealing with change and loss carefully and prayerfully. Consider using it as a resource for your own information. Or, if you work with seniors, incorporate some of the material into an evening of reflection on the good-byes they face.

Media connections

- Explore the cultural phenomenon of death denial. Using magazine ads and TV commercials, have the young people find items that promise to slow aging, regrow hair, recapture youthful exuberance, and so forth. Discuss society's discomfort with the topic of death and its fixation on eternal youth.
- Check out *www.textweek. com, www.teachwithmovies. org,* and *www.hollywood jesus.com* for lists of movies on the session theme. Check out the ratings, the commentary, and the connections to the theme, and decide what is appropriate for your group.

VARIATION:
Gender Groups

Discuss with the young people how easy or difficult it is for each gender to express certain emotions. For example, in many areas it is culturally more acceptable for males to express emotions like anger and passion than emotions like tenderness and fear. It is the opposite for females. Talk about the cultural pressures and the dangers of suppressing feelings.

The Category Is . . .

Group 1	• Students Against Drunk Driving (SADD) • language club • mock trial	• basketball team • marching band • student council
Category:		
Group 2	• sleep in late • go to a party • do homework	• attend Sunday Mass • help with chores at home • hang out with friends
Category:		
Group 3	• laugh • argue • hug	• apologize • cry • withdraw from everyone
Category:		
Group 4	• drinking alcohol • running away • getting violent	• eating too much or too little • hurting oneself • taking unnecessary risks
Category:		
Group 5	• changing schools • a sudden illness • graduation	• getting cut from a team • the separation of parents • getting a part-time job
Category:		

Changes and Losses in My Life

Nothing endures but change.
(Heraclitus, c. 540–c. 480 B.C.)

A significant change I recently experienced is . . .

Because of that change, I lost . . .

From that change, I learned . . .

I still have questions about . . .

Something positive that came out of the change is . . .

The things that got me through the difficult times were . . .

(The quote from Heraclitus is taken from John Bartlett's *Familiar Quotations,* sixteenth edition, edited by Justin Kaplan [Boston: Little, Brown and Company, 1992], page 62, copyright © 1992 by Little, Brown and Company.)

Words of Comfort

Those who wait for the LORD shall renew
their strength,
they shall mount up with wings
like eagles,
they shall run and not be weary.
(Isaiah 40:31, NRSV)

To you, O LORD, I lift up my soul.
O my God, in you I trust.
(Psalm 25:1–2, NRSV)

Do not be afraid, for I am your God;
I will strengthen you, I will help you.
(Isaiah 41:10, NRSV)

For God alone my soul waits in silence,
for my hope is from [God].
(Psalm 62:5, NRSV)

Do not fear, for I have redeemed you;
I have called you by name, you are
mine.
(Isaiah 43:1, NRSV)

Trust in [God] at all times, O people;
pour out your heart before him;
God is a refuge for us.
(Psalm 62:8, NRSV)

Because you have made the LORD your
refuge,

. . . .

no evil shall befall you.

(Psalm 91:9–10, NRSV)

If I take the wings of the morning

. . . .

even there your hand shall lead me,
and your right hand shall hold me
fast.

(Psalm 139:9–10, NRSV)

Whey they call to me, I will answer them;
I will be with them in trouble,
I will rescue them and honor them.

(Psalm 91:15, NRSV)

"Blessed are those who mourn, for they
will be comforted."

(Matthew 5:4, NRSV)

My help comes from the LORD,
who made heaven and earth.

(Psalm 121:2, NRSV)

"Come to me, all you that are weary and
are carrying heavy burdens, and I will give
you rest."

(Matthew 11:28, NRSV)

"I am with you always, to the end of
the age."

(Matthew 28:20, NRSV)

"I am the light of the world. Whoever
follows me will never walk in darkness
but will have the light of life."

(John 8:12, NRSV)

"For nothing will be impossible with
God."

(Luke 1:37, NRSV)

"Peace I leave with you; my peace I give
to you. . . . Do not let your hearts be
troubled."

(John 14:27, NRSV)

By the tender mercy of our God,
the dawn from on high will break
upon us,

. . . .

to guide our feet into the way of
peace.

(Luke 1:78–79, NRSV)

"My grace is sufficient for you, for power
is made perfect in weakness."

(2 Corinthians 12:9, NRSV)

God will fully satisfy every need of yours according to his riches in glory in Christ Jesus.

(Philippians 4:19, NRSV)

[God] will wipe every tear from their eyes.

. . . .

Crying . . . will be no more.

(Revelation 21:4, NRSV)

Overview

Learning to communicate effectively is important in all relationships. For parents and teenagers, being able to communicate effectively is the key to peaceful living and healthy growth. Effective communication and problem solving are means to handle the changes and disruptions that occur regularly in family life, because they help parents and teens recognize that the needs and roles of family members change over time and that their relationship must adapt accordingly. The foundations of effective communication are respect, recognizing motivations, and listening to understand rather than to respond.

Special Considerations

Sessions on communication are helpful for everyone in every relationship. However, if a relationship is strained or unhealthy, a session such as this one can open up the proverbial can of worms and further harm the relationship. Also, family situations vary widely, as does parent availability for and interest in sessions such as these. Be sensitive to teens that do not live with both parents, teens that are struggling in their relationships with their parents because of abuse or addictions, and teens whose parents cannot or choose not to attend a session such as this one. You might want to invite some adults who can connect with teens whose parents are not available. You might also suggest that teens invite a parent or another significant adult in their lives, such as a grandparent, another relative, a Confirmation sponsor, or a mentor.

A Note About Time

This session is designed to fit into a 1-hour time frame, like all the other sessions in this manual. However, we strongly encourage you to extend this session by using some of the options listed in the Try This sections for each activity. Doing that will offer both teens and their parents more opportunities to practice their skills and connect with each other.

Outcomes

◆ The participants will identify issues that often cause conflict between parents and teenagers.

◆ The participants will discuss the motives behind people's requests and responses.

◆ The participants will explore empathic listening as a key ingredient of effective communication.

Background Reading

◆ Scriptural connections: Sir. 3:1–16 (duties toward parents), Eph. 6:1–4 (honoring each other), Col. 3:18—4:1 (rules for Christian households)

◆ *Catholic Youth Bible* article connections: "Ravens and Vultures" (Prov. 30:17), "Honoring Our Parents in God's Way!" (Sir. 3:1–16), "Family Relationships" (Eph. 5:21—6:4)

Core Session: Listening to Understand (60 minutes)

Preparation

• Gather the following items:

❑ newsprint

❑ markers

❑ masking tape

❑ blank paper

• Make a sign with the word "Easy" on it, and another with the word "Difficult" on it. Post the signs at opposite ends of the room.

• List the following topics on newsprint:

  ○ family issues and home life

  ○ school activities

  ○ sexuality

  ○ friends

  ○ social life, including dating

  ○ clothing and other appearance choices

  ○ faith and religion

  ○ community and world events

- ○ drugs, alcohol, smoking
- ○ emotions
- Recruit an observer to take note of difficult issues identified by the participants in step 2 of the focusing activity.

Focusing and Discussion: Parent-Teen Issues (20 minutes)

1. Welcome the young people and their parents. Affirm their presence, noting that it indicates a real commitment to building stronger relationships with each other. No matter how strong a relationship is to begin with, focused attention can only make it stronger. Explain the direction and purpose of this session, and encourage the young people and their parents to participate fully.

2. Ask the participants to stand in the middle of the room. Point out the two signs at the opposite ends, and explain that they represent the two ends of an imaginary continuum. Announce that you will read a number of topics. After each one, they are to move to the point on the continuum that indicates how easy or difficult it is for parents and teens to communicate about that topic.

Announce each of the topics that you listed on newsprint, and allow time for the participants to move. Do not engage the group in conversation about the topics. Instruct the observer to make note of the topics that people seemed to think were most difficult to discuss.

3. Invite the participants and the observer to offer their comments about communication, referring to the continuum exercise and noting the most difficult topics. Ask them to name other issues, and add those to the newsprint list.

4. Divide the participants into mixed groups of five or six teens and parents. Give each group two sheets of newsprint and markers. Assign each of the groups one of the more difficult communication topics from the list. Explain that the groups are to do three things:
- Clearly identify the issue—the what, when, where, why, who, and how of the situation.
- Suggest motivations from the perspectives of both parents and teens. In other words, identify what it is about this topic that makes communication difficult and may even cause conflict. For example, if the issue is social life and dating, the motivation for teens may be independence and social connections. The issue for parents may be safety and maturity. List the motivations on a sheet of newsprint, in separate columns for parents and teens.

VARIATION:
Large Group

Instead of using a continuum post the numbers 1 through 10 around the room. Have the participants move to the number that represents the level of comfort felt when discussing each of the proposed topics.

Try This

- ◆ If the group is small or if you have extra time, recruit volunteers to role-play the top three issues identified by the group. After each role-play, work with the participants to identify the issues and the obstacles.
- ◆ Use two continuums—one for parents and the other for teens. Tell the observer to note differences and similarities in the two groups' perceptions of various communication topics.

- Name the obstacles to effective communication that often arise, such as lecturing or name-calling. List them on the second sheet of newsprint, in separate columns for parents and teens.

    Allow about 10 minutes for the groups to work; then direct them to post their lists. Group the motivations lists on one part of a wall and the obstacles lists on another.

Presentation: Obstacles to Communication (10 minutes)

Review the posted lists of motivations and obstacles, commenting on items that are repeated. Make the following points in your own words, referring to the list of obstacles and noting your observations about obstacles that are missing from the list:

- The motivations for teens and parents are rooted in human development and experience. It is normal and healthy for young people to want to achieve independence, make social connections, and pursue interests. It is natural and necessary for parents to be concerned about physical and emotional safety, maturity level, and balance. The communication difficulties that often arise are a result of a conflict of motivational priorities.

- To add to the difficulty, people often create obstacles to effective communication in these twelve ways:

    ○ Judging, criticizing, and blaming: "You don't trust me!"
    ○ Name-calling, ridiculing: "You are *so* immature!"
    ○ Interpreting, diagnosing: "You're just jealous of . . ."
    ○ Praising (in a patronizing way), agreeing: "Well, I think you're . . . (pretty, smart, a good player, and so forth)."
    ○ Ordering, directing, commanding: "Don't ever talk to me like that!"
    ○ Warning, admonishing, threatening: "If you do that, you'll be sorry."
    ○ Exhorting, moralizing, preaching: "You ought to . . ."
    ○ Excessive or inappropriate questioning: "Why do you suppose you hate . . ."
    ○ Advising or giving solutions: "Go make friends with someone else."
    ○ Diverting, distracting: "Why don't you just try doing something different, like playing the tuba?"
    ○ Lecturing, teaching, giving logical arguments: "Let's look at the facts."
    ○ Reassuring, sympathizing: "Don't worry, things will work out fine."
    (Adapted from Robert Bolton, *People Skills*, pp. 15–16)

- Avoiding the obstacles to communication allows both parties to hear each other in a nonconfrontational manner. By doing so, they may be able to understand the motivations more clearly and arrive at a mutually acceptable solution.

TryThis

◆ Give each small group from the focusing activity a list of the twelve ways that people create obstacles, and have them brainstorm examples of each one. Invite them to share the examples with everyone. After the session, compile the examples and send them to the participants.

◆ Using the assigned communication topics have each small group develop a role-play in which parents and teens reverse roles and practice using the obstacles. Then have them assume their appropriate roles and have them do the role-play again, taking care to avoid the obstacles.

Discussion and Presentation:
Elements of Effective Communication (20 minutes)

1. Divide the participants into small groups of parents only and teens only. Give each group a sheet of newsprint and markers. Explain that the groups are each to make a list of at least three key ingredients for effective communication that they would like the other group to use. In other words, the teens are developing key ingredients for the parents, and the parents are doing the same for the teens. For example, one ingredient might be "listening more than you talk." Another might be "not jumping in before a person is finished with a thought." Allow about 10 minutes for the groups to compile their lists.

Post the lists, and give the participants a chance to review them. Invite brief comments.

2. Ask the participants if they know where the following sentence comes from:

Divine Master,
grant that I may not so much seek . . .
to be understood as to understand.

If they cannot identify the source, reveal that it is from the peace prayer attributed to Saint Francis of Assisi, a prayer about ways to foster peace between individuals.

Make the following points in your own words:

○ In order to really listen, stop talking! You can't listen while you're talking.

○ Empathize with what the other person is saying. Imagine what it might mean to be in that person's position.

○ Ask open-ended questions (questions that require more than a yes or no response) about the person's life.

○ Observe the body language of the other person, and be aware of your own. Your body language can send a message that inhibits good communication. Think about how it feels to talk to someone who has his or her arms crossed and the kind of message that sends.

○ Eye contact is a good way to let others know that you are paying attention. However, in some cultures eye contact is considered offensive.

○ Listen carefully to the other person, and try to feed back to that person what you are hearing. This is a way of letting the person know that you understand what she or he is saying. If something is unclear, ask for more explanation.

○ Take care to listen to the facts and to the emotions that are connected to the conversation. Often the emotions will say much more than the facts.

TryThis

◆ If time is running short, simply note that part of effective communication is good listening, which means listening to understand the other person rather than to respond.

◆ You may want to model a conversation using the good listening skills with one or more of the participants. If you choose to do that, practice it before the session.

○ The goal of good and effective listening is greater understanding, rather than solutions.

○ It takes time and practice to develop the skill of good listening. Don't give up . . . just keep practicing.

(This activity is adapted from *YouthWorks* [Naugatuck, CT: Center for Ministry Development, 1994], p. 5.)

Conclusion: We Believe . . . ; We Will . . . (10 minutes)

1. Ask the participants to return to the small groups they were in for the previous activity. Give each small group a sheet of paper. Tell the groups to think of all they talked about during the session, and to develop two statements summarizing what they learned and what action they will take. The first statement should begin with the phrase "We believe," and the second with "We will." Allow about 5 minutes for the groups to do their work.

2. Invite a representative of each small group to read the group's statements. Conclude by reading the "Prayer of Saint Francis," which can be found on pages 384–385 of *The Catholic Faith Handbook for Youth.*

Pray It

Instruments of Peace (15 minutes)

Preparation
- Gather the following items:
  - ❑ a candle and matches
  - ❑ copies of handout 12, "The Peace Prayer Attributed to Saint Francis: A Responsive Reading," one for each participant
  - ❑ a *Catholic Youth Bible* or other Bible
  - ❑ the "We believe . . ." and "We will . . ." statements from the closing activity of the session
  - ❑ a recording or score of the "Prayer of Saint Francis" (optional)
- Set up a prayer table with a candle and a Bible. You might also want to add a statue or depiction of Saint Francis of Assisi.
- Recruit one parent and one teen to proclaim Eph. 6:1–4.

◆ If you had the participants do role-plays earlier in the session, have them present their situations again using the skills of good listening. Remind them to *seek first to understand* and *then to be understood.*

TryThis

Replace step 2 with the prayer service that appears in the Pray It section that follows.

Try This

◆ You may want to have the participants write their statements as part of this Pray It activity. This can be done in small groups, in family groups, or individually. At the start of the activity, distribute index cards and pens or pencils. After the reading from Ephesians, direct the participants to write their statements. As they read the statements, they should put them on the prayer table.

◆ Use three different sets of readers for the three proclamations of Eph. 6:1–4.

Media connections

Videotape several scenes from popular television shows and movies that depict parents and teens communicating. Play each scene, and discuss from a parent's perspective and a teenager's perspective how realistic it is, the obstacles to communication, good communication techniques, and so on.

1. Gather everyone around the prayer table and light the candle. Distribute handout 12, "The Peace Prayer Attributed to Saint Francis: A Responsive Reading." Call the participants to become silent inside and out. After a moment, invite the scriptural readers to come forward. The teen reader should proclaim Eph. 6:1–3, followed by the parent proclaiming Eph. 6:4. You may want to suggest that they change the word *fathers* to *mothers and fathers* or to *parents*.

2. Invite a representative from each of the previous activity's small groups to read the group's "We believe . . ." statement. Then invite the scriptural readers to proclaim the reading again, this time reversing the parts. Finally, invite another representative from each small group to read the group's "We will . . ." statement.

3. Divide the large group in half, and designate side 1 and side 2. Read the prayer on handout 12 as it is outlined.

4. Invite the scriptural readers to proclaim Eph. 6:1–4, this time reading it in unison. If it is available, conclude by singing or playing a recording of the "Prayer of Saint Francis." It is included in the *Spirit & Song* collection as well as in other parish hymnals.

LIVE it!

Options and Actions

- **Family communication declaration.** Have the participants work in family groups to develop a list of "We believe . . ." and "We will . . ." statements. Suggest that this list be posted in a key location in the home. The participants may want to make copies for every member of the family.
- **Peace prayer.** Divide the participants into small groups. Assign each group a section of the "Prayer of Saint Francis," which can be found on pages 384–385 of *The Catholic Faith Handbook for Youth.* Instruct the groups to discuss how the section applies to keeping peace in families, especially between parents and teens.
- **Empathic listening.** Develop an entire session on empathic listening for parents and teens, allowing them opportunities to hear more about the concept and to practice the skills. Information on the topic can be found in Stephen R. Covey's *The Seven Habits of Highly Effective People: Restoring the Character Ethic* (New York: Simon and Schuster, 1989).

- **Reconciliation.** As a follow-up to this session or as part of a longer session, conduct a reconciliation service for teens and parents in the parish. It could be a prayerful time, allowing each to say, "I'm sorry," and to make a promise to improve the relationship.
- **Life cycle.** As part of the session, include a presentation on the life cycle and how human beings grow and change throughout life. Focus on the developmental issues that are particular to adults in midlife and to adolescents. Doing so may help teens and their parents understand each other a little more.
- **Are we communicating?** At the beginning of the session, play a game of "telephone." Direct the participants to sit in a circle. Whisper a sentence to one person. Each person repeats in a whisper to the next person what she or he hears. After the statement has made it around the circle, check to see how accurate the final result is.
- **Closing reflection.** At the end of the session, give the participants a chance to reflect on or discuss the following sentence starters:
  ○ I learned that . . .
  ○ I still have questions about . . .
  ○ I hope that . . .
  ○ I will use what I have learned in the coming week by . . .
- **Scriptural advice.** Lead the participants in a study of Sir. 3:1–16. Discuss questions such as these:
  ○ What advice does Jesus Ben Sira give to mothers? to fathers? to children?
  ○ What special blessings are in store for family members?
- **Parented by all.** Use the *Catholic Youth Bible* article "Honoring Our Parents in God's Way!" near Sir. 3:1–16, to help young people think about the people who parent them, but who are not related to them biologically.

VARIATION:
Gender Groups

Use the *Catholic Youth Bible* articles "Words from a Mother to Her Daughter!" and "Words from a Father to His Son!" near Wisdom of Solomon, chapter 12, as the basis for separate gender-based sessions. Include time for parents to discuss with their children wisdom they gleaned from their own parents that they want to pass on, and time for the teens to discuss the wisdom they want to pass on to their own children.

JournalACTIVITIES

- What is something you know about one of your parents now that you did not know last week?
- What is one thing you would like to say to one of your parents?
- What are some things you are willing to do to build the relationship between you and your parents?

The Peace Prayer Attributed to Saint Francis: A Responsive Reading

Side 1

Make me an instrument of your peace.
Where there is hatred, let me bring love;
Where there is injustice, your pardon, Lord;
And where there is doubt, true faith in you.

Make me an instrument of your peace.
It is in pardoning that we are pardoned,
In giving of ourselves that we receive,
And in dying that we are born to eternal life.

Make me an instrument of your peace.
Where there is despair in life, let me bring hope;
Where there is darkness, only light;
And where there is sadness, ever joy.

O Master, grant that I may never seek
So much to be consoled as to console,
To be understood as to understand,
To be loved as to love with all my soul.

Side 2

Help me to receive and convey your peace.
Let me replace my hatred with love.
When I have been unjust, let me ask for pardon.
And when I doubt, Lord, let me share the strength
of another's faith.

Help me to receive and convey your peace.
Let me ask for forgiveness so that others may
know the joy of forgiving.
Let me receive the gifts of others with gratitude so
that they may know the joy of sharing.
And let me join with others in dying and rebirth.

Help me to receive and convey your peace.
When I am filled with despair, let me look at your
creation and be filled with hope.
When I live in darkness, let me search for light in
friendship and love.
And when sadness colors my days, help me to
find joy in knowing I am loved.

O Master, grant that I will always seek
To console and to understand another's need to
offer consolation,
To understand and to appreciate another's efforts
to understand me,
And to live fully, giving and receiving love with all
my soul.

(This prayer is adapted from Gail Daniels Hassett, *Parent-Teen Relationships* [Winona, MN: Saint Mary's Press, 1996], page 42, copyright © 1996 by Saint Mary's Press, all rights reserved.)

11

Helping Peers in Crisis

AT A GLANCE

Study It

**Core Session:
Hurtful Times,
Helpful Friends**
(60 minutes)

◆ Focusing:
The Weight of the World
(20 minutes)

◆ Presentation and
Discussion: Knowing
What to Look For
(20 minutes)

◆ Discussion:
What Can I Do?
(20 minutes)

Pray It

◆ Burdens in a Bundle
(15 minutes)

Live It

◆ Learning to listen
◆ Suicide prevention
◆ Where to go for help
◆ Job's troubles
◆ Depression knockouts

Overview

Difficulty is part of everyone's life—we cannot avoid it. Sometimes we are able to deal with our struggles and move on. Other times we need a little extra help to overcome the difficulties, and occasionally we find ourselves facing crises because of them. Our closest friends are often our first line of defense when life becomes too much to handle alone. This session builds on teens' natural tendency toward relationship, and gives them some tools to help friends who are struggling.

A Special Consideration

As a response to this session, young people who are in crisis or who have a friend who is in crisis may want to talk to someone about the situation. You may want to have a few extra adults present in case they are needed.

Outcomes

◆ The participants will understand that everyone has difficult times, and that for some people, difficulties may result in a crisis.
◆ The participants will learn the warning signs of a friend who is headed for trouble.
◆ The participants will learn what they can do to help a friend who is in crisis.

Background Reading

◆ Scriptural connections: Job 2:11–13 (Job's friends), Job 7:1–11 (Job's suffering), Psalm 23 (God's care)
◆ *Catholic Youth Bible* article connections: "Suicide Is Not an Answer" (1 Sam. 31:1–7), "Facing the Hard Times" (Mark 15:16–20)

Study
it!

Core Session:
Hurtful Times, Helpful Friends
(60 minutes)

Preparation

- Gather the following items
  - ❑ a sheet of poster board or foam board, or a plastic garbage bag
  - ❑ four identical chairs, buckets, or similar items
  - ❑ heavy-duty masking tape or duct tape (optional)
  - ❑ a variety of objects of different weights and sizes, such as pieces of wood, rocks, balls, books, stuffed animals, and so forth
  - ❑ a *Catholic Youth Bible* or other Bible
  - ❑ copies of handout 13, "Knowing What to Look For," one for each participant
  - ❑ newsprint
  - ❑ markers
  - ❑ copies of handout 14, "What Can I Do?" one for each participant
- Suspend the poster board, foam board, or plastic bag between the four chairs or buckets, forming a makeshift table with only the four corners of the "tabletop" in contact with the "legs of the chair." Secure the top with tape if necessary.

Focusing: The Weight of the World
(20 minutes)

1. Gather the young people around the makeshift table. Announce that you will read a story about the ups and downs in the life of a teenager. Explain that you will pause periodically and ask someone to choose an item that represents the seriousness of each situation and place it on the makeshift table.

2. Read the following story. Feel free to change some of the details so that they apply to your local situation. Pause at each set of ellipsis points, and invite someone from the group to add an item to the table. You may not get through the whole story before the table collapses, but finish reading it anyway.

- It's Friday night. James and his friends are trying to decide what to do for the evening. His friend Mitch would have had some great ideas, but Mitch

TryThis

Instead of using a makeshift table, recruit a volunteer to stand in front of the group and be the recipient of the items. At some point the person will not be able to carry anything else, and may drop everything. Add the following question to the discussion: "What could (name of person) have done with all the things he was carrying?" The answer you want to elicit from the group is that the person could have asked for help instead of carrying it all alone.

and his family moved across the country a few months ago. Everyone misses Mitch, especially James. . . . James wants to make it a good evening. It's the first Friday he's been able to go out since he was grounded by his dad after a major argument about—well, just about everything. . . . James and his dad haven't been getting along well lately. It seems like every time they're together, they fight. . . . Being at his mom's house isn't much better. He doesn't get along with his stepdad, and it's worse when his kids are there for the weekend. He always takes their side. . . . Sometimes James feels like he doesn't belong anywhere. . . . He has often thought that no matter what anyone says, divorce is hardest on the kids. He knows that from experience. . . .

His school life isn't much better. He has a huge chemistry test coming up. He has a C average in chemistry—not enough to get him into college as a preveterinary major, that's for sure. His teacher told James that she knows he can do better, and she offered to help him. He never took her up on the offer. . . . His grades aren't much better in American literature and global studies. Both of his parents are constantly pressuring him to study. It seems they're not satisfied with anything but A's. . . . James doesn't care much anymore, though. He's got other things on his mind. . . .

It's not been the greatest year for James. Besides the divorce and his best friend moving, there was Katie, his girlfriend for six months. James thought things were going well—until one day Katie told him she thought they should see other people. . . . Two days later, James saw Katie at a party. She was with one of his friends. Well, his *former* friend. . . . Nothing was right after that. James just couldn't get Katie out of his mind. . . .

Then there was—well—"the incident." James doesn't talk about it much, but he knows he messed up *big* time, and every time he thinks about it, he gets a sinking feeling in his stomach. . . . He did it on a dare one night. He was drunk—something that's been happening more and more since he started hanging around with a new bunch of guys, who live for weekend parties. . . . James goes along whenever he can. It's better than staying home with his stepfather's bratty kids. . . . Anyway, one night the guys saw a car running in the parking lot of a convenience store. They dared James and another guy to hop in the car and take it for a short ride. The two took them up on the dare. . . . It was either that or be ridiculed. . . . .The other guy drove; James went along for the ride. They only went about three blocks when the car slammed into a tree. James got out and tried to run, but the cops were right there. . . . He's never seen his parents so angry. . . . He has a court date coming up. . . .

James has been doing a lot of thinking lately. It seems like everything is going wrong. . . . He can't seem to do well at anything. . . . He does things he *knows* he shouldn't do. . . . He can't seem to have a decent conversation with either of his parents. . . . He's always wanted to be a veterinarian, but he doubts that it will happen with the nosedive his grades have taken. . . . He doesn't feel like he belongs anywhere anymore. . . . And he doesn't feel like anyone really cares. . . . James has been doing a lot of thinking lately. . . .

3. Lead a discussion in the full group of the following questions:
- What are some of James's problems?
- How is he handling his problems?
- The last line of the story is, "James has been doing a lot of thinking lately. . . ." What do you think James has been thinking about?

Presentation and Discussion: Knowing What to Look For (20 minutes)

1. Read Rom. 8:26. Ask the young people to think about a time when things were going so badly for them that they could not even find the words to talk about it or pray about it—times when they were capable only of "sighs too deep for words." Allow a moment for reflection.

2. Make the following points in your own words, incorporating the young people's comments and observations from the previous activity:
- Everyone has bad days, or even a few bad days in a row. They are part of being human, just as the good days are. We usually recognize them for what they are—temporary setbacks, speed bumps along the road of life. Most of the time, we deal with our problems and move on.
- Sometimes people get to a point where they are overwhelmed by life's difficulties and need help. That situation could be due to many factors, including these:
  - They may be dealing with a series of difficult situations that just keep piling on top of everything else.
  - They may have recently experienced the loss of a significant person in their life through death, divorce, or the end of a relationship.
- Sometimes depression sets in, a condition that is highly treatable with professional help. Most people act out in some way when they are depressed. Friends may be the first ones to recognize the signs and encourage them to reach out for help.

3. Distribute handout 13, "Knowing What to Look For." Reread the story about James from the previous activity. Point out the warning signs on the handout, and ask the young people to identify the ones that James exhibited.

Review all the signs, emphasizing these points:
- Look for changes in regular behavioral patterns, not one or two isolated incidents.

- Some signs indicate the need for immediate help. Those include revelations about abuse or suicidal thoughts. The last two items on the handout —a sudden recovery from depression and the dispersal of possessions —often indicate that the person has made a decision to harm herself or himself.

- People who struggle with a history of abuse, chemical dependency, or an eating disorder need particular and immediate help.

Discussion: What Can I Do? (20 minutes)

1. Divide the teens into small groups of four or five participants. Explain that they are to discuss the following question:

- If you were James's friends, what could you have done to help him?

Allow about 8 minutes for the discussion; then have each group give a report. Write their responses on newsprint.

2. Distribute copies of handout 14, "What Can I Do?" Compare the participants' responses with the points listed on the handout. Emphasize the three major points:

- *Listen.* Listening is the most caring thing one person can do for someone who is hurting. What matters most is that you are there.
- *Ask.* Trust your feelings and instincts. Be direct.
- *Tell.* Do not allow yourself to be sworn to secrecy. Tell an adult—a parent, a coach, a teacher, a counselor, a youth minister, or someone else you trust. It is better to damage a friendship than to lose a friend.

3. Close by reading the passage from Job 2:11–13 from handout 14. Encourage the young people to be there for one another in times of distress, and to reach out for help when their own burdens become too great. Affirm God's love and compassion for each of us, all the days of our lives.

Burdens in a Bundle (15 minutes)

Preparation

- Gather the following items:
  - ❑ a *Catholic Youth Bible* or other Bible
  - ❑ a candle and matches
  - ❑ 6- or 8-inch squares of cloth, one for each participant
  - ❑ one copy of resource 6, "Placing Our Burdens in a Bundle," cut apart as scored

Mediaconnections

- ◆ Check out *www.textweek. com, www.teachwithmovies. org*, and *www.hollywood jesus.com* for lists of movies on the session theme. Check out the ratings, the commentary, and the connections to the theme, and decide what is appropriate for your group.

- ◆ Many Web sites provide good information on teen crises, and include multiple links to other sites. Here are two helpful Web sites on teenage suicide prevention:
  - ◇ *www.yellowribbon.org*
  - ◇ *www.darkmother.com/ nosuicide.html*

- ◆ Invite the teens to bring in music with lyrics that speak of despair, hopelessness, and pain. Lead a discussion about reaching out for help and the role of faith and hope in dealing with such feelings.

***Spirit & Song* connections**

- ◆ "Be Not Afraid," by Bob Dufford
- ◆ "God's Eye Is on the Sparrow," by Bob Hurd

Try This

Instead of using cloth squares, you might provide brown paper bags and small pebbles to symbolize burdens. Adolescent boys—particularly younger ones—might see the fabric squares as too feminine. And younger teens in general might appreciate the concreteness of small stones to represent burdens.

- Set up a prayer table with a Bible, a candle, and the squares of cloth.
- Recruit five readers, and give each one a segment of resource 6.

1. Gather the teens around the prayer table. Light the candle; then give each person one of the fabric squares. Explain that the participants are to lay the cloth in their lap and concentrate on it while you lead them through a short meditation. Read the following meditation, pausing briefly at each set of ellipsis points:

- This small square of cloth that you have in your lap is unique. It can hold anything and everything you want to put in it. . . . It seems small, but it's as big as your soul, as limitless as God. . . . Think about the burdens that you carry with you: . . . difficulties in your family, . . . problems with your friends, . . . pressures at school, . . . questions about your future, . . . struggles, . . . anything at all that causes fear, loneliness, doubt, or pain. . . . Imagine yourself placing those burdens into the cloth one by one. . . .

  Tie together the opposite corners of the cloth to form a small bundle. . . . Hold the bundle in the hollow of your hands. . . . Lift it up from your lap. . . . Feel its lightness. . . . Now imagine yourself handing this bundle to God, . . . and imagine God taking it from you . . . completely understanding every burden that you've put in it. . . . Continue to hold your bundle as we pray our intercessions.

2. Invite the readers to pray aloud, in turn, their intercessions from resource 6. Announce that the group response to each intercession is, "God, hold us in your hands." After the five intercessions have been read, encourage the participants to add their own intentions. Respond as a group after each one.

3. Encourage the teens to take their bundles home and keep them in a prominent place. Suggest that they take the bundle from that place during overwhelming and discouraging moments, open it, and imagine that they are placing another burden in it. After doing so, they should retie the bundle and give it to God, just as they did today.

Conclude by reading Matt. 11:28–30.

(This activity is adapted from Marilyn Kielbasa, *Prayer,* pp. 62–64.)

Options and Actions

- **Learning to listen.** Lead a session on communication skills for teens that will help them help others. Focus on the skills of listening actively, responding with accurate empathy, giving feedback, and so forth.

- **Suicide prevention.** Invite a speaker from a community-based suicide prevention program to talk to the group about the suicidal process and how to recognize the signs that a friend is considering suicide.

- **Where to go for help.** Gather phone books and information about help lines, hotlines, and mental-health agencies. Have the young people create a composite list of the resources available in the area, and distribute the list to all the families in the parish.

- **Job's troubles.** Lead the young people in studying Job 7:1–11 and how Job's description of sadness and depression applies to them or to someone they know. For a detailed plan, see the session "Sadness and Depression" in *ScriptureWalk Senior High Discipleship: Bible-Based Sessions for Teens,* by Nora Bradbury-Haehl (Winona, MN: Saint Mary's Press, 2000), pages 59–65.

- **Depression knockouts.** Brainstorm with the young people a list of things to do to battle the blahs or mild depression. The list might include actions like these:
  - Bake bread from scratch or make a batch of cookies.
  - Go to a comedic movie.
  - Take a warm bath or a cold shower.
  - Fix or build something.
  - Exercise.

Familyconnections

- The book *Adolescents in Crisis: A Guidebook for Parents, Teachers, Ministers, and Counselors,* by G. Wade Rowatt Jr. (Louisville, KY: Westminster John Knox Press, 2001), is a helpful resource for youth leaders and for parents who have troubled teens at home.

- Collect books, videos, and audiotapes, and build a pastoral-care library in the parish, where parents can find information about the issues their teenagers face, such as substance abuse and depression.

JournalACTIVITIES

- Write about a time when things were going so badly for you that all you could muster were "sighs too deep for words" (Rom. 8:26).

- Have you ever helped a friend through a tough time? Has anyone ever helped you? Write about what you have learned about yourself and about the helping process.

Knowing What to Look For

Your friend **may** need help if he or she . . .

- has trouble concentrating
- doesn't care about declining grades
- loses interest in things that mattered before
- takes dangerous risks
- withdraws from others
- experiences a change in eating or sleeping patterns
- starts drinking or taking drugs
- becomes promiscuous
- is suddenly getting into a lot of fights
- has unexplainable mood swings
- exhibits changes in behavior or performance

Many of those signs are particularly significant if they represent a change in behavior. For example, if a person is a natural risk taker, a risky action is probably not a cause for concern if everything else is in balance. A person who is naturally introverted may withdraw from others on a regular basis to recharge her or his energy. Look at the whole picture, but if you're not sure, err on the side of caution.

Your friend **definitely** needs help if she or he . . .

- reveals a deep sense of hopelessness, despair, or rage
- discloses that she or he has been or is being abused or has been raped
- tells you that she or he is addicted to drugs or alcohol
- talks or writes about suicide
- shares with you her or his struggles with an eating disorder
- suddenly recovers after a long period of depression
- gives away prized possessions

What Can I Do?

When Job's three friends heard of all these troubles that had come upon him, each of them set out from his home. . . . They met together to go and console and comfort him. . . . They sat with him on the ground seven days and seven nights, and no one spoke a word to him, for they saw that his suffering was very great. (Job 2:11–13)

Job's friends responded to his troubles by just being with him. What they did is an important first step, though it can be hard to just *be* there with a friend. Sometimes we feel helpless. Once we have established a caring presence, the following steps are important.

Listen

Listen to your friend. Try to understand what he or she is feeling. Reflect back what you hear. Show your care and support. Offer words of comfort, and a hug if the person seems open to it. Do not try to minimize your friend's problems by comparing them with your own or someone else's.

Ask

If you think your friend is in crisis, trust your feelings. If you suspect your friend is suicidal, be direct: "Are you considering suicide?" You will not put the idea in your friend's head by suggesting it. If you think your friend is contemplating a risky behavior that will harm him or her, share your concern. If it seems your friend is trying to tell you something but can't come right out and say it, share your suspicion and ask for clarification: "Are you trying to tell me that you think you're an alcoholic?" "Are you saying that someone is abusing you?" "Do you think you might be pregnant?" Your friend will probably be relieved that the words came out of your mouth, not hers or his.

Tell

It is important that you tell an adult what is going on. The adult might be a teacher, a counselor, a parent, or someone at church. That person should be able to get your friend the help that he or she needs. Of course, if the situation is immediately dangerous, stay with your friend while he or she or you call a crisis hotline or 911. Whatever you do, do *not* let yourself be sworn to secrecy. Your friend may be angry with you for telling someone, but it's better to damage the friendship than to lose the friend.

Placing Our Burdens in a Bundle

Reader 1: For all those who do not believe in their own goodness and holiness, and for those who feel they have nowhere to turn, we pray . . .
All: God, hold us in your hands.

Reader 2: For those who are sick in body, mind, or spirit, that they may know God's healing touch in their most painful moments, we pray . . .
All: God, hold us in your hands.

Reader 3: For the acceptance of diversity in all its forms—in schools, in society, and in the Church—we pray . . .
All: God, hold us in your hands.

Reader 4: For all those who help others as counselors, companions, and friends, we pray . . .
All: God, hold us in your hands.

Reader 5: For the burdens we hold in our hands here today, that we may know that we are not alone in our struggles, we pray . . .
All: God, hold us in your hands.

(This resource is adapted from Marilyn Kielbasa, *Prayer: Celebrating and Reflecting with Girls* [Winona, MN: Saint Mary's Press, 2002], page 65, copyright © 2002 by Saint Mary's Press, all rights reserved.)

12

Sexuality and Spirituality

Overview

The focus of this session is helping young people realize the God-given gift of sexuality as an integrated part of their spirituality, a part of who they are from the moment of conception until the moment of death. The purpose of this session is to help them understand the concept of sexual integrity as the ideal way to achieve the fullness of life of which Jesus speaks. They will also think about setting boundaries in their relationships to help them achieve that goal.

Special Considerations

Keep in mind that each young person in your group is likely to have different levels of experience and even interest. To assume that all are sexually involved or that all are virgins is both limiting and dangerous. Be open and nonjudgmental about what you see and hear. Do not be afraid to hold up the good news that God is calling us to love more deeply, more respectfully, and more unselfishly, and to lead lives of fullness and integrity.

Outcomes

◆ The participants will explore the concept of sexual integrity as a way to achieve fullness of life.
◆ The participants will learn about setting boundaries and making appropriate choices for evolving stages of relationships.

Background Reading

◆ Scriptural connections: Gen. 1:26–31 (the creation of human beings), Song of Sol. 2:1–17 (a tribute to sexuality), Eph. 5:1–8 (Renounce sinful ways.), 1 Thess. 4:1–8 (a life pleasing to God)
◆ *Catholic Youth Bible* article connections: "A Fresh Start" (Psalm 51), "Living Well" (1 Cor. 6:12–20), "True Love Waits" (1 Thess. 4:1–8)

Study It

Core Session:
Achieving Sexual Integrity
(60 minutes)

◆ Focusing:
Human Beings,
Sexual Beings
(15 minutes)
◆ Presentation and
Discussion: Relating
with Integrity
(15 minutes)
◆ Continuum:
Physical Intimacy
Timeline
(20 minutes)
◆ Reflection:
I Learned, but I Wonder
(10 minutes)

Pray It

◆ Holy of Holies
(15 minutes)

Live It

◆ APPLE prints
◆ Just say no
◆ True Love Waits
◆ Sexuality education series
◆ Second chances

Core Session:
Achieving Sexual Integrity (60 minutes)

Preparation
- Gather the following items:
  - ❑ 3-inch-by-3-inch squares of paper in two different colors, one color for boys and the other for girls, three squares for each participant
  - ❑ markers
  - ❑ blank paper
  - ❑ masking tape
  - ❑ one copy of resource 7, "Sexual Integrity," enlarged
- Create signs with the following words and phrases on them, and post the signs along one wall or along the floor to form a continuum:
  - ○ hanging out
  - ○ group dating
  - ○ individual dating
  - ○ going steady
  - ○ engagement
  - ○ marriage

Focusing: Human Beings, Sexual Beings (15 minutes)

1. Give each person three squares of paper and a marker; use a different color of paper for girls and boys. Explain that you will read three questions. After each question, the participants are to write an answer on a square of paper, large enough so that it can be seen throughout the room.

2. Read each of the following questions, and allow time for the teens to write their answers:
- At what age do most people realize that their bodies are different from those belonging to people of the other gender?
- At what age do most people become sexual?
- At what age do most people become self-conscious about their bodies?

3. Read each question again, and ask the teens to hold up their answers. Do a quick assessment of the general trend for each gender, and offer comments. Point out that the correct answer for the second question is the

TryThis

- ◆ Collect the papers after each question, keeping the answers from the girls and the boys separate. Have someone average the answers and present a group composite.

same for both girls and boys because we are all sexual beings from the moment we are conceived. Invite reactions from the young people.

4. Make the following points in your own words, inviting questions or comments from the young people:

- Sexuality is part of who you are, made in the image of God. You are a sexual being from the moment you are conceived until the day you die.
- Sexuality is much more than sexual acts, sexual intercourse, or sexual behavior. Sexuality is not what you do—it is who you are.
- Sexuality is a part of all your relationships with others. It plays a role in your relationships with people who are your age and with those who are older and younger. It plays a role in your relationships with people of the other gender, as well as those of your own gender.
- Sexuality is intimately connected with your spirituality, your relationship with God.

Presentation and Discussion: Relating with Integrity (15 minutes)

1. Display the enlarged copy of resource 7, "Sexual Integrity," and refer to it as you make the following points:

- The word *integrity* comes from the root word *integer,* which means "whole" or "complete." For someone to be a person of integrity, their attitudes and actions must reflect all aspects of the whole person God created him or her to be.
- Both spirituality and sexuality are part of every aspect of our beings: our minds, hearts, and bodies. None of those aspects can be separated from the others. We are whole and integrated beings, made in the image of God.
- Sexual integrity has the following three dimensions. Together they make up the fullness of human sexuality for which we were created.
  - ○ physical pleasure
  - ○ procreation of life
  - ○ expression of total commitment

2. Lead a discussion of the following questions:

- If a couple engage in sexual activity for one or two of the three reasons listed in step 1, what are the implications? What are the results?
- Why, do you think, does the Church teach that sexual intercourse is appropriate only within the context of marriage?

Be sure to cover these points in the discussion:

- If someone engages in sexual activity simply for pleasure, that person is using her or his partner. Even if both parties agree, they are ignoring the emotional and spiritual dimensions of sex.

◆ Before asking each gender group to reveal its answers, ask the other gender group what they think its answers will be.

◆ Before beginning the presentation, ask the young people to offer completions to the sentence starter "Sexuality is . . ." List their responses on newsprint, or have them write anonymous responses on paper. Collect the papers and read them aloud.

- If someone engages in sex for the sole purpose of conceiving a child, the act does not require emotional intimacy or love.
- If someone engages in sexual activity only as a way to express commitment and not for pleasure, the act is more martyrlike than meaningful.
- It is common for two people to engage in sexual activity in pursuit of pleasure and as an expression of love. However, that leaves out the procreative aspect. Although not every act of sexual intercourse results in new human life, the possibility is always there. People who are not willing to accept and nurture the new life that may result do not have the kind of committed love that the sexual act was intended to express.
- The Church recognizes that sex is a sign of sacramental love, a particularly profound encounter with God through our spouses. The Church also speaks of procreation and the joy and pleasure of sex within the context of marriage.

Continuum: Physical Intimacy Timeline (20 minutes)

1. Ask the young people what they think of when they hear the phrase "intimate relationship." Their responses will likely refer to sexual intimacy. Explain that intimacy takes many forms. Two people can be intimate emotionally, intellectually, and spiritually, as well as physically. In a healthy, committed relationship, all levels of intimacy are approximately the same. This is what is known as relational integrity. Becoming physically intimate with someone without also being spiritually and emotionally intimate with that person at the same level can bring about tremendous pain for both people.

2. Direct the young people to stand in the middle of the room, facing the signs you have posted. If necessary, come to a common understanding of the types of relationships indicated by the signs, so that for instance, everyone understands what "hanging out" and "going steady" mean.

Explain that you will read a number of actions. The young people are to move to the point on the continuum where they consider that action to be appropriate for the first time. For example, holding hands is appropriate during most of the timeline, but may first be appropriate at the group dating stage.

Use the first five actions in the following list, and as many others as you have time for:
- hugging
- touching intimately over clothes
- having sex
- making genital-to-genital contact
- holding hands

TryThis

- Before beginning the timeline activity, ask the young people to brainstorm a list of sexual actions and behaviors.
- You may want to add a discussion of "red, yellow, and green zones" to help clarify the appropriateness of an activity along the continuum:
  ◇ Green zones indicate activities and behaviors that are safe in the sense that they do not necessarily lead to intimate activity.
  ◇ Yellow zones signify behaviors that need a lot of caution. These are occasions of serious temptation.
  ◇ The red zone is where things get hot! Partners are aroused, and it is very hard to stop. To preserve sexual integrity, activities in the red

- saying "I love you"
- kissing heavily
- giving back rubs
- kissing casually
- having a baby

Allow time for discussion and observations. In particular, look for and comment on the following reactions:

- a wide variety of responses from the teens regarding the appropriateness of a particular action
- different responses from each gender regarding an action
- responses that are not in line with the Church's teaching
- responses that the young people agree on, but that you know are wrong if one is to maintain sexual integrity

3. Close the activity by making the following comments in your own words:

- A good question to keep asking is, "How does this particular action bring a couple to a holier, healthier, respectful, and growth-filled relationship at this particular level?"
- In the privacy of your own prayer life and in mutual conversation with your partner, you will need to use your properly formed and informed conscience to make a decision about where to draw the line. It is easiest to do so if both partners are equally committed to maintaining sexual integrity.
- The most well-thought-out plan can go awry if a person is under the influence of alcohol or other drugs. Making good decisions about peer groups, recreational activities, and the people you spend time with alone are all important to setting boundaries.

Reflection: I Learned, but I Wonder (10 minutes)

1. Invite the young people to think about something they learned in the session and something they still wonder about. Encourage them to voice their learnings and their wonderings aloud.

2. Conclude by reading 1 Cor. 6:19–20. If time allows, lead the prayer service "Holy of Holies," which follows.

zone should be reserved for the permanent, committed relationship of marriage.
(Adapted from Janet Claussen with Julia Ann Keller, *Seeking,* p. 117)

VARIATION:
Small Groups

If you have a large number of participants and extra time, divide the young people into small groups. Give each group a list of levels of relationships and a set of sexual activities and behaviors. Allow each group to create its own time-line. Bring the groups together to create a final version that authentically reflects sexual integrity.

TryThis

Many young people may be reluctant to voice the questions they still have about sexuality. Provide paper, and ask the teens to write their learnings and wonderings, but not to sign their names. Read some of the statements aloud.

Holy of Holies (15 minutes)

Preparation

- Gather the following items:
  - ❑ three *Catholic Youth Bibles* or other Bibles
  - ❑ three candles and matches
- Designate three points around the room as prayer points. Place a Bible and a candle at each point.
- Recruit three volunteers to read the following passages:
  - ○ 1 Cor. 6:12,18–20
  - ○ Gen. 1:26–28
  - ○ Song of Sol. 8:6–7

1. Explain that the Temple of Jerusalem at the time of Jesus had three main rooms: the vestibule, where people entered; the holy place; and the holy of holies, a small room deep within the Temple that was entirely empty and totally dark. The high priest alone entered the holy of holies, and only for the most sacred reasons and occasions. It was separated from the holy place by a veil.

Ask the participants how the image of the holy of holies in the Temple connects with sexuality.

2. Ask the participants to turn to the first prayer point. Light the candle and call the first volunteer to read 1 Cor. 6:12,18–20. Invite the young people to reflect on the following comment and questions:

- If our bodies are like temples, the most intimate parts of us—physically, psychologically, and spiritually—are like the holy of holies, sacred places to be approached with reverence and awe.
  - ○ In what ways do you already show reverence and awe for your body?
  - ○ Knowing that your sexuality is part of the holy of holies in your temple, how will you honor that part of your being?

3. Ask the participants to turn to the second prayer point. Light the candle and call the second volunteer to read Gen. 1:26–28. Invite the young people to reflect on the following comment and questions:

- When God created human beings, they were naked. However, now, in almost all cultures, men and women cover their genitalia, just like the veil over the holy of holies. Men and women cover their genitalia not because sex is dirty, but because it is holy. The parts of the body that they cover are the ones that contain the secret of generating and sustaining life.

○ How can clothing inspire reverence for the human body? How can it inspire lust?

○ What does your clothing say about your attitude toward your body?

4. Ask the participants to turn to the third prayer point. Light the candle and call the third volunteer to read Song of Sol. 8:6–7. Invite the teens to reflect on the following comment and questions:

• The Song of Solomon is an entire book devoted to the love between two people, their attraction to and desire for each other. The book speaks of the goodness of human sexuality and the beauty of human love. Its inclusion in the Bible teaches us that sexuality and love are gifts from God, things to be celebrated and used within God's plan.

○ Have you ever thought of sex as holy? Why or why not?

○ What is your attitude toward sexual activity if you truly consider it to be a gift of God?

5. Close with a challenge to think carefully about sexuality as one element of the holy of holies in the temple that is one's body. Invite three people to blow out the candles.

(This activity is adapted from Janet Claussen with Julia Ann Keller, *Seeking*, pp. 118–119.)

Options and Actions

• **APPLE prints.** Slice an apple in half across the middle. Show the participants the five-pointed star formed by the seeds. Use the acronym *APPLE* to explain the following five points about sexuality:

○ **A**ccept your sexuality as God's gift.

○ **P**repare yourself for sexual decision-making.

○ **P**ray about sexuality and relationships.

○ **L**imit yourself; don't count on the other person to set sexual limits.

○ **E**xpect respect; don't settle for less.

Give the participants index cards or half-sheets of card stock. Suggest that they each create a miniposter of the acronym. Make poster paints available so that the teens can decorate their posters with prints of star shapes from the apple halves.

Mediaconnections

Challenge the young people to watch one evening of prime-time television and to note the depictions of and references to sexual situations. Suggest that they evaluate the shows through the lens of sexual integrity.

Catholic Faith Handbook connections

In the *CFH*, chapter 27, "Respecting Sexuality," offers a thorough presentation of Catholic moral teachings on the topic of sexual morality.

Familyconnections

◆ Using the material in this session, conduct a session for parents and teens on the topic of sexual integrity. Encourage the teens to present some of the material and lead the activities.

◆ Compile and send home a bibliography of good resources on the topic of teens and sexuality, along with questions and ways to start the conversation between parents and teens.

◆ Encourage parents to watch television with their teens, and to discuss the sexual values portrayed in popular shows. Provide a format for evaluation, such as the following questions:

◇ What messages do you feel, hear, or see about women? men? the body? relationships? sex? love?

◇ What values are being expressed?

JournalACTIVITIES

◆ In your Bible, read Song of Sol. 2:1–17. Choose a phrase or two that really speak to you, and write them in your journal.

◆ What is holy about sex?

◆ In your mind, what is the difference between sex and sexuality?

◆ If you found out that someone you cared for deeply was sexually active, what would you say to that person?

• **Just say no.** Ask the young people to come up with lines that people use to pressure someone into having sex, such as: "You would if you loved me," "Everyone else in our group has done it," and "We can't stop now; you've got me too excited." After they brainstorm the lines, ask them to develop possible ways to say no. You may want to do this in gender groups.

• **True Love Waits.** This program is a national ecumenical initiative for youth that promotes abstention from sexual intercourse and other sexual activity before marriage. The Catholic version of TLW is available through the National Federation for Catholic Youth Ministry at *www.nfcym.org*. Click on "programs."

• **Sexuality education series.** Use this chapter as the basis for a series on sexuality. Include sessions on Church teaching, pregnancy, abortion, chastity, homosexuality, masturbation, and media censorship. You may want to survey the young people to see what topics they would most like to hear about. Include guest speakers, videos, and other media. Your diocesan office likely has a wide variety of resources. Check with your pastor and the diocesan office about guidelines for conducting sexuality education programs.

• **Second chances.** Read the following scenario to the group. Discuss with the young people how they would answer the questions that this person poses at the end of the story.

> I met him at a party, and it was love at first sight! We didn't stop talking all night. After that, he asked me out the next weekend, and the next and the next. We took walks. We held hands. We talked about everything and anything. We kissed.
>
> About three months after we started dating, we went to the beach. Afterward we went to my house to change because we were going to meet some friends that evening. No one was home. We started to make out. Before I knew it, we were having sex. I was scared and surprised. I think he was too.
>
> We didn't want it to happen, but it did. He wants to be alone with me all the time now. I keep telling him that I don't want to have sex, but he insists that because we've already "lost it," we may as well enjoy it. Sometimes I let him, but I don't really want this to be what our relationship is about. Is my life ruined? Is his? What should we do?

Use the story of the penitent woman from Luke 7:36–50 to help the teens understand that Jesus forgives and insists on giving us a second chance at making things right.

Sexual Integrity

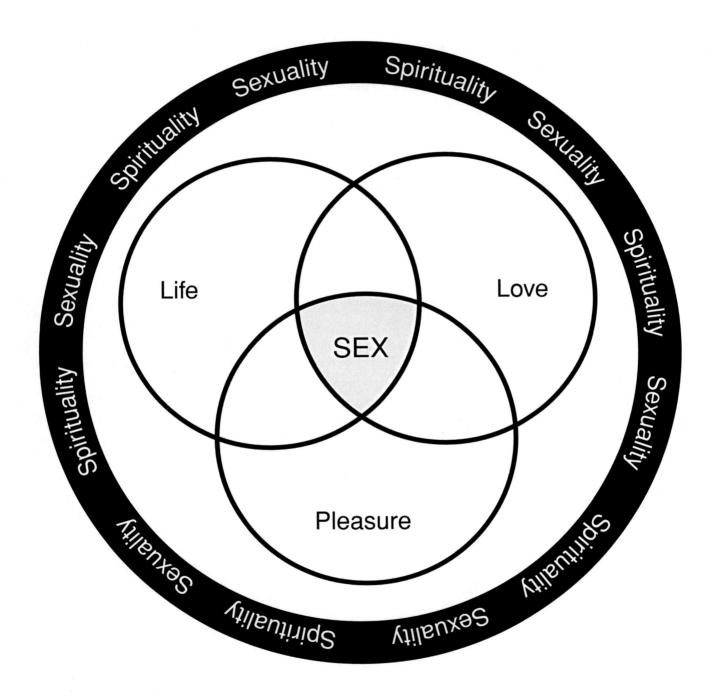

(This resource is from Janet Claussen with Julia Ann Keller, *Seeking: Doing Theology with Girls* [Winona, MN: Saint Mary's Press, 2003], page 129, copyright © 2003 by Saint Mary's Press, all rights reserved.)

13 Finding Hope

Overview

Hope is a "theological virtue by which we desire and expect from God both eternal life and the grace we need to attain it" (*CCC,* p. 882). The road to eternal life includes both fresh, smooth pavement, and potholes that make our journey bumpy and treacherous. Hope gives us the patience to endure and the courage to see the gift in it all. Young people often feel hopeless, especially when they get to the potholes in the road. They lack life's experience of finding the smooth pavement again. They often confuse happiness and hope, and may see faith as something totally separate. This session is about helping the young people see the connections between happiness, hope, and faith, and the role those elements play in bringing them closer to eternal life. It also helps them recognize internal and external sources of hope that they can draw on when needed.

Outcomes

- The participants will compare the Gospel's image of happiness with contemporary culture's image of happiness.
- The participants will explore the connection between faith, hope, and happiness.
- The participants will reflect on sources of hope in their lives.

Background Reading

- Scriptural connections: Psalm 14 (a denunciation of Godlessness), Rom. 8:18–30 (future glory), Heb. 6:19–20 (the certainty of God's promise)
- *Catholic Youth Bible* article connections: "Hope" (Rom. 8:18–30), "Hopeless and Hurting" (2 Cor. 4:16–18), "Anchor of the Soul" (Heb. 6:19–20)

Core Session:
Hopeful, Faith-full, and Happy
(60 minutes)

Preparation

- Gather the following items:
  - ❑ newsprint
  - ❑ markers
  - ❑ inexpensive prizes (optional)
  - ❑ *Catholic Youth Bibles* or other Bibles, one for each participant
  - ❑ copies of handout 15, "Finding HOPE," one for each participant
  - ❑ pens or pencils
  - ❑ a recording of reflective music and the appropriate equipment (optional)
- Recruit four readers, and assign each reader one of the following passages:
  - ○ Luke 4:4–9
  - ○ Luke 4:13–17
  - ○ Luke 4:22–26
  - ○ Luke 4:32–34

Focusing and Discussion: True Happiness
(20 minutes)

1. Divide the young people into small groups. Give each group a sheet of newsprint and markers. Direct the groups to list fifty things to be happy about. You may want to present the task as a competition, and award inexpensive prizes to the members of the first group that lists fifty things.

2. Give the groups the following instructions:
- Circle three items from the list that give lasting happiness.
- Cross off three items that give false or temporary happiness.
Invite the groups to share their lists and the highlighted items with everyone.

3. Call the readers to proclaim the passages from Luke's Gospel. Then lead a discussion using the following questions:
- What does Jesus say about true happiness?
- How does society's idea of happiness compare with the concepts found in Luke's Gospel?

TryThis

If you have extra time available, distribute Bibles and divide the teens into four small groups. Assign each small group one of the passages from Luke's Gospel, and direct it to explain what Jesus is saying about happiness.

JournalACTIVITIES

◆ Where do you find hope? What people, activities, or ideas give you the courage to carry on when you are going through a difficult time? Make a list of your sources of hope, and mark it in such a way that you can find it easily the next time things look bleak.

◆ Write a letter to a friend who is sinking into despair and hopelessness. What would you tell that person about hope?

◆ Complete this statement: I feel hopeful when . . .

• Do most people you know seek happiness in the ways identified in those passages? Explain.
• What is the connection between happiness and hope?

4. Make the following comments in your own words:
• One of the major themes of Luke's Gospel is joy and happiness. Chapter 12 is a series of warnings against the pitfalls that keep us from true happiness, the things that might hold us back from pure joy.
• Chasing after things that cannot provide true happiness is something people have probably done since the beginning of time. They certainly did so in Jesus' time, as this passage in Luke's Gospel attests.
• Jesus is not saying that finding true happiness is an easy thing. Seeking true happiness means putting people before possessions. It means trusting in God over relying only on our own efforts.
• *Happiness* and *hopefulness* are not synonyms. A person can be hopeful even though happiness is elusive. In fact, hopefulness is one sign of a person that has a deep faith. That person knows that no matter what happens, God is there—and God is the source of all hope.
• History plus hope equals happiness. We *know* that we have experienced happiness before. Even when things are not going well, we remember that somewhere in our history, we knew the feeling of pure joy that comes only from God. And when that feeling is not there, we hope—that is, we have faith—that it will come again, just as God promised.
• Happiness is a state of mind. It is the fulfillment of a promise. Hope is the virtue that sustains us along the road. The basis of hope is faith: faith that the God who created us is always present to us; faith that through his Resurrection, Jesus is the fulfillment of God's promise and the source of eternal hope; and faith that God's Spirit is with us constantly, filling us with the grace to recognize the source of true happiness.

(This activity is adapted from Nora Bradbury-Haehl, *Scripture Walk Senior High Discipleship*, pp. 43–44.)

Discussion: Making Connections (20 minutes)

1. Divide the young people into groups of three or four. Assign each group one of the following passages, and ask the groups to interpret what the passages say about faith, hope, or happiness.
• Heb. 2:12–13
• Heb. 6:19
• Heb. 11:1
• Heb. 11:39

2. Give each group a sheet of newsprint and markers. Explain that the groups are to discuss the relationship between faith, hope, and happiness, and to come up with an image that symbolizes the connection between the three concepts. You might offer suggestions such as these:

- Hope is the car we drive. Faith is the fuel. Happiness is the road ahead.
- Faith is the camera. Hope is the film. Happiness is the resulting photograph.
- Faith is the wax of a candle. Hope is the burning wick. Happiness is the warmth the candle produces.

State that the groups should draw a picture of their symbols and prepare to explain the analogies to everyone. Allow about 7 or 8 minutes for the small groups to complete those tasks.

3. Invite each group to share its analogies with everyone. Conclude by emphasizing that faith in God is the foundation on which hope is built. Hope is the gift of sustained energy. Happiness is the fulfillment of the promise of hope.

Reflection: Finding HOPE (20 minutes)

1. Offer the following sentence starters, and invite the young people to answer spontaneously:

- In tough times, hope is . . .
- In good times, hope is . . .

2. Distribute handout 15, "Finding HOPE," and pens or pencils. Explain that sustaining God's gift of hope takes determination and energy on our part. We need to rely on resources within us and outside us—all part of God's gift of HOPE:

- **History.** Remembering that we have survived and grown through tough times gives us hope that we will do so again.
- **Others.** Looking to others for support, encouragement, honesty, and laughter gives us hope that we're not alone.
- **Prayer.** Turning to God in prayer, looking to the Scriptures and Catholic Tradition for comfort, and sharing our faith with others means that we share in the hope of the Resurrection.
- **Enthusiasm.** We each have things we are enthusiastic and passionate about that fill our souls, gradually displacing the emptiness and filling it with hope. Those are our sources of true happiness.

Thinking about those things when we are in a good place can help us the next time our situation looks bleak.

3. Invite the young people to move to a comfortable place where they can be alone with their thoughts. You may want to play reflective music if it is available. Allow about 10 minutes for the teens to write their thoughts on the handout.

TryThis

- Instead of drawing a picture, have the small groups dramatize the image in some way. You may want to provide props and other resources.
- As an alternative or a prelude to this activity, write each of the following sentence starters on a sheet of newsprint:
  ◇ Hope is . . .
  ◇ Faith is . . .
  ◇ Happiness is . . .
  Invite the young people to complete the sentences. Use their answers as the basis for a discussion of the relationship between the three gifts.

TryThis

In small groups, have the young people identify other elements that fit with the acronym *HOPE*. For example, instead of "enthusiasm" they might use "enjoyment" or "energy." List all the alternatives for each letter on newsprint. During the reflection time, invite the young people to choose one word for each letter, and identify their personal sources of hope that correspond to it.

4. Suggest that the teens keep the completed handout in a place where they can easily get to it if life begins to unravel. Close by reading Lam. 3:22–24, a passage of profound hope in a book rooted in profound grief.

PrayIt

My Greatest Hope (15 minutes)

Preparation

- Gather the following items:
  - ☐ copies of handout 16, "My Greatest Hope," one for each participant
  - ☐ pens or pencils
  - ☐ a *Catholic Youth Bible* or other Bible
  - ☐ three candles and matches
  - ☐ a recording of a song about hope, preferably one that is joyful and up-beat, and the appropriate equipment (optional)
- Recruit three readers for the following scriptural passages:
  - ○ Jer. 29:11
  - ○ Ps. 31:21–24
  - ○ Tob. 13:6–8
- Set a prayer table in the middle of the group, and place a Bible and three candles on it.

1. Gather the participants around the prayer table. Give each person a copy of handout 16, "My Greatest Hope," and a pen or a pencil. Comment that everyone holds deep inside a great hope for themselves, for family and friends, and for the world. Explain that the young people will have the chance to voice their own hopes during this prayer time. Tell them to spend a few quiet moments completing the sentence starters on the handout.

2. Ask the first reader to proclaim Jer. 29:11 and to light one candle. Then invite the young people to read in random order their completed statements that begin with "My greatest hope for myself is . . ." Assure them that they do not have to read their statements if they do not wish to do so.

Follow the same process with each of the other scriptural passages and reflection statements. Close with a song about hope if you chose one before the session.

Spirit & Song connections

- "How Can I Keep from Singing," attributed to Robert Lowry
- "Lord of All Hopefulness," by Timothy R. Smith
- "O Taste and See," by Marty Haugen

TryThis

To keep the teens' thoughts anonymous, collect the handouts and recruit a reader for each set of statements. After each scriptural reading, invite the statement reader to begin sharing the sentence completions. If you have a large group, have each volunteer read only some of the statements.

Options and Actions

- **How do you spell *faith?*** Discuss the meaning of faith as it is described in Heb. 11:1. Then facilitate the exercise in the *Catholic Youth Bible (CYB)* article connected with the passage.

- **Dialogue on believing.** Recruit two volunteers to read the dialogue between God and an angel in the article "Believing," near Psalm 14 in the *CYB.*

- **Hope hunt.** Assign the young people the task of finding as many symbols of hope as possible before the next gathering. Examples are an acorn, a newspaper story about a cure for an illness, a picture of a group of children playing together, and a sign from a peace demonstration. Explain that the teens should take a notebook or a camera to make note of anything that cannot be brought to the group.

- **Hope in the Scriptures.** Have the young people use a Bible concordance to identify all the times the word *hope* appears in the Scriptures. Discuss the role of hope in the lives of our ancestors in faith.

- **Hope quotes.** Provide books of quotations and index cards. Encourage the young people to write their favorite quotes about hope on the cards, and keep them in a place where they can find them easily. They may want to decorate the cards and use them as bookmarks, or perhaps make a set and pass them along to family and friends who are in need of a bit of encouragement or hope.

- **Festival of hope.** Work with the teens to plan a festival of hope for the parish. The festival might be held in mid-winter, a time of struggle for many people, especially older people. It could include live music with songs on the theme of hope, seed planting, spring flowers, a hope collage, crafts, games, and movies on hopeful themes.

- **Spreading hope.** Use the festival idea above, but do it in a series of visits to a nursing home or an adult day-care center. Do one or two activities on each visit.

- **Children's stories of hope.** Many children's stories are based on hope leading to happiness. Have the young people read several such stories and discuss whether the happiness is based on Gospel values or cultural values. Have them write reviews of some of the books for the parish bulletin or newsletter.

Familyconnections

- ◆ Send home handout 15, "Finding HOPE," with directions to discuss each element as a family and to look for ways that family members can support one another during difficult times.

- ◆ Suggest that families use a "hope candle" at times when they are all together, inviting their members each to offer things that they are hoping for, are hopeful about, or see as signs of hope. The younger members of the family might use decorating tools to write the word *hope* on the candle.

- ◆ Encourage parents to share their thoughts and stories of hope with their teens. Such sharing will help teens realize that everyone hopes for something and everyone has times in their life when they need to draw on internal and external sources of hope.

Mediaconnections

Check out *www.textweek. com, www.teachwithmovies. org,* and *www.hollywoodjesus. com* for lists of movies on the session theme. Check out the ratings, the commentary, and the connections to the theme, and decide what is appropriate for your group.

Finding HOPE

H = **History**

Identify times in your life when you felt hopeful even though you were struggling, times when something or someone helped pull you through, and times when you knew there was a light in the darkness.

O = **Others**

List the names of people with whom you can share your struggles, people who bring a smile to your face, and people who encourage you to keep on going when things look bleak.

P = **Prayer**

List some favorite prayers, poems, or scriptural passages in which you find hope. Also list the names of people with whom you can pray and comfortably share your faith.

E = **Enthusiasm**

List the places, people, activities, and pursuits about which you are enthusiastic, the things you enjoy doing, and other ideas to fill your soul when you feel empty and hopeless.

My Greatest Hope

My greatest hope for myself is . . .

My greatest hope for my family and those I love is . . .

My greatest hope for the world is . . .

Part C

Strategies for Effective Pastoral Care of Youth

Pastoral Care of Youth

Positive Youth Development

Chapter 1 of this manual, "Pastoral Care and Youth Ministry," lists five key principles:

- Pastoral care is not counseling.
- Pastoral care goes beyond crises.
- Pastoral care is everyone's responsibility.
- Pastoral care must help youth develop life skills.
- Pastoral care must address the needs of families.

This chapter proposes twelve proven strategies that are rooted in those five principles. When employed strategically and consistently, the strategies provide preventive pastoral care for adolescents and their families.

Strategy 1: Promoting Positive Values

If young people are to develop a solid foundation on which to build their lives and become healthy, contributing members of the Church and the community, Gospel values such as compassion, honesty, integrity, human dignity, and equality need to be promoted. A first step in implementing that foundation is evaluating the Church's ministry to young people, including all youth ministry and religious education programming, to discover the values that are being communicated. Consideration should be given to these goals:

- Address young people as whole, multidimensional human beings.
- Teach them to be people of integrity.
- Challenge them to discipleship.
- Proclaim the Good News and invite them to embrace it.

Strategy 2: Life-Skills Training

One of the most significant ways to promote positive youth development is to create intentional programs and activities that develop the life skills of adolescents. Among the skills they need are how to make decisions, how to

TryThis

Check out these articles in *The Catholic Youth Bible* for scriptural connections to promoting positive values:

- ◆ "Kwanzaa as a Way of Life" (Deut. 10:12–22)
- ◆ "Stand Up!" (Bar. 4:17–19)
- ◆ "Consistent and Trustworthy" (Gal. 2:11–14)
- ◆ "Living Gospel Values Even if It Demands Suffering!" (1 Pet. 3:13–22)

TryThis

Check out these articles in
The Catholic Youth Bible for
scriptural connections to
promoting life skills:
- ◆ "Integrity and Values"
  (Psalm 26)
- ◆ "Decide!" (Psalm 62)
- ◆ "Called to Follow Jesus"
  (Mark 1:16–20)
- ◆ "Christian Community"
  (Acts 2:43–47)

TryThis

Check out these articles in
The Catholic Youth Bible for
scriptural connections to
promoting Christian living:
- ◆ "You Shall Be Holy"
  (Leviticus, chaps. 19–20)
- ◆ "Media Literacy"
  (Prov. 1:10)
- ◆ "What Goes Around"
  (Obadiah, v. 15)
- ◆ "Fill Me, Lord"
  (Gal. 5:22–26)

communicate with others, how to make friends, how to stand up for what they believe, and how to resolve conflicts nonviolently. Adolescents need to learn to take responsibility and to exercise self-control. They also need opportunities to deal directly with important adolescent struggles and to discuss those issues and the feelings they generate.

Life-skills training should aim at developing the following areas:
- strong perceptions of personal capabilities
- strong perceptions of significance in primary relationships
- strong perceptions of personal power
- strong intrapersonal skills
- strong interpersonal skills
- strong systemic skills, such as responsibility and adaptability
- strong judgment skills

Every parish and school should sponsor life-skills training as an integral part of youth ministry and religious education programming. Using the sessions in this manual is a good start, but many opportunities exist for further development. Investigate what other churches, schools, and youth organizations in your community are already doing. Possible approaches include these:
- Facilitate community-building activities that build trust and relationship among participants.
- Organize youth-group meetings on community, relationships, and friends.
- Hold prayer services on acknowledging gifts and affirming others.
- Provide personal development workshops on recognizing gifts and talents, friendship-making skills, decision-making skills, and listening skills.

Strategy 3:
Constructive Activities That Promote Christian Living

Young people need to be involved in activities that address diverse needs and interests. Youth ministry programming, including catechesis, needs to address the developmental needs of youth and consciously promote their internal assets. Activities that engage young people in contributing to the community, where they can learn new skills and put their faith into action, should be high on the list of every church's youth ministry program, as should opportunities for reflective silence and meaningful prayer.

Among the skills young people need to develop are practical skills for living the Christian faith in the world today, which will allow them to challenge people and systems that promote values that are contrary to the Gospel. Those include skills in critical thinking, which will help them to honestly and incisively critique all forms of media. Youth should also be given the tools to think independently of the prevailing culture and to question all systems effectively. Possible approaches include these:

- Develop media literacy among young people; check out the Center for Media Literacy's Web site, *www.medialit.org.*
- Work with organizations such as Habitat for Humanity that offer skill building in addition to working with and for others in the community.
- Take advantage of liturgical seasons, especially Advent and Lent, to provide opportunities to engage in critical reflection.
- Use movie trailers, which can easily be found online, as a starting point for a discussion about Christian values that may or may not be present in the movies. Check Web sites such as Teach with Movies *(www.teachwith movies.org)* and Ministry and Media *(www.ministryandmedia.com)* for suggestions on using movies with young people.

Strategy 4: Opportunities for Meaningful Service

Self-esteem has two parts: self-worth and self-efficacy. Self-worth has to do with feeling good about oneself. Self-efficacy describes the sense that one can effect change, that one's individual actions can impact people, policies, and institutions.

Service is an excellent way to build self-esteem, develop Gospel-based values in young people, and promote their growth in faith. Every youth ministry program should provide a well-organized community service component that includes education, action, and reflection, and that responds to a variety of interests. That component might include local service projects as well as plug into established diocesan, regional, and national programs. Service to God's people should be promoted as a way of life—not simply a "project."

In addition to developing youth-specific service programs, identify which parish groups are engaged in service (in its broadest sense), and work with them to include youth in their present and future programs. Work to ensure that reflection is a part of service experiences and service learning. The Total Youth Ministry manual *Ministry Resources for Justice and Service* provides guidance for developing service involvements for youth and for providing justice education. Possible approaches to service include these:

- Connect young people with parishwide service opportunities.
- Provide seasonal listings of service opportunities that are available in the parish and the wider community.
- Invite representatives of various service organizations to come and speak with the young people about service opportunities.
- Coordinate a "Do It Justice" event, providing young people and parishioners with resources and ideas for creating a more just and peaceful community and world.

TryThis

Check out these articles in *The Catholic Youth Bible* for scriptural connections to promoting justice and service:

- "The Gospel Call to Conversion" (Matt. 7:21–27)
- "Jesus and Civil Disobedience" (Matt. 21:12–13)
- "The Miniature Gospel" (Matt. 22:34–40)

TryThis

Check out these articles in
The Catholic Youth Bible for
scriptural connections to promoting leadership:

◆ "Perseverance
   in Leadership"
   (2 Chron. 32:27–33)
◆ "Courage" (Psalm 31)
◆ "Leaders with Character"
   (Prov. 6:16–19)

TryThis

Check out these articles in
The Catholic Youth Bible for
scriptural connections to
pastoral care for those who
are most vulnerable:

◆ "Love and Jealousy"
   (Gen. 16:1–16)
◆ "Hagar's Rescue"
   (Gen. 21:8–21)
◆ "We Are the Body of
   Christ!" (Rom. 12:1–8)

Strategy 5:
Training Youth Leaders and Utilizing Their Skills

Every person has the potential for leadership, and will likely be called on to exercise that role at some point in life. Communities owe it to young people to provide training in the skill sets required for effective leadership: communication, visioning, team building, and planning, to name just a few.

By engaging young people in leadership roles in the school or parish community, you build consistent involvement and create a sense of ownership among the teens. Think about the possibilities for leadership in the ministries, programs, and activities of the parish, in addition to the youth ministry program. Connect young people with leadership opportunities for parish events, service opportunities, and children's religious education programs. Besides building leadership skills, it is a great way to build mentoring relationships between adults and youth in the community. The Total Youth Ministry manual *Ministry Resources for Leadership* provides leadership training sessions and helpful ideas for including youth in leadership roles. Possible approaches to leadership include these:

- Provide opportunities for leadership formation, including personal development and skills training.
- Talk with parish ministry leaders about incorporating young people into leadership roles.
- Develop a mentoring program that recruits youth to mentor children in the parish's faith-formation program or as tutors in local Catholic schools.

Strategy 6: At-Risk Concerns

No matter who they are, where they live, what their family's economic status is, or what their academic record looks like, many teens face choices and have to make decisions about activities that put them at risk for life-altering consequences. Some teens are at greater risk than others, depending on a variety of factors.

It is essential that all ministers (and parents) face the realities of life in the twenty-first century, and assist teens in building a foundation that will help them stay strong when confronted with tough choices. High-risk youth in impoverished communities especially need social support networks. Provide information and educational programs about issues such as sexual activity, violence, and substance abuse, and connect those issues with Christian values. Provide contact information for hotlines and help lines. Many school districts and mental-health agencies have resource people who conduct programs on those topics. Investigate other churches, schools, hospitals, and youth organizations in the community to see what is already happening in your area. Possible approaches to helping at-risk youth include these:

- Work with parents in encouraging the formation of covenants and pledges to not drink and drive.
- Develop the social skills of adolescents by involving them in support groups and teaching them appropriate behavior.
- Develop a recommended list of counselors and treatment centers.

Strategy 7: Opportunities to Contribute to Parish Life

Young people need to feel valued and accepted by the community. They need to know that they can assume meaningful roles within the life of the community, which can provide experiences of real responsibility. Such roles enhance young people's sense of purpose, and nurture feelings of belonging and loyalty to the community. They also provide opportunities to develop intergenerational relationships, which are important for sharing faith and promoting growth.

Meaningful involvement of young people is the responsibility of the entire community. Leaders in ministry with youth must advocate for youth participation in leadership, service, community life, liturgical ministries, and seasonal preparations. The Church must provide adequate training, practice, and guidance for young people in public roles so that they succeed—in their own eyes as well as in the eyes of those who scrutinize their involvement. Possible approaches to youth participation include these:

- Talk with the liturgy director about incorporating young people in the liturgical ministries—as hospitality ministers, lectors, altar servers, Eucharistic ministers, and musicians.
- Meet with leaders of parish groups and organizations to identify ways for young people to be connected with their work and activities.
- Encourage the participation of young people on the parish pastoral council and in endeavors such as Disciples in Mission and small Christian communities.

Strategy 8: Caring and Supportive Adult-Teen Relationships

Adolescents need caring, consistent adult relationships beyond those with their parents. They need meaningful contact with adults with whom they can have in-depth conversations and to whom they can go for advice and support. Every parish can nurture such relationships through mentoring and intergenerational programming.

To be effective, mentors must be persistent and resourceful. They must find ways to build trust that fit the particular individual they are mentoring and the cultural context in which they are working. They should know how to set tangible, usually modest goals early in the relationship. They must know how to empathize with a developing adolescent: to be reasonably

TryThis

Check out these articles in *The Catholic Youth Bible* for scriptural connections to promoting parish involvement:
- "Prophets of Hope, Youth on a Mission!" (Eph. 4:17–32)
- "Training for Christ" (1 Tim. 4:7–10)
- "Part of the Family" (1 Pet. 2:9–17)

TryThis

Check out these articles in *The Catholic Youth Bible* for scriptural connections to promoting mentoring relationships:
- "Friends" (Sir. 6:5–17)
- "Children and Green Trees" (Jer. 17:1–3)
- "I Give God Thanks for You!" (Eph. 1:15–23)

sensitive to what is current, what is likely to be credible, and how to make sense of the adolescent experience.

For young people's protection, extreme care should be taken when recruiting adult volunteers and mentors. Most diocesan offices have a prescribed process for engaging the services of people to work with children and teens. Provide training for mentors and ongoing opportunities for feedback and support. Possible approaches to building mentoring relationships include these:

- Develop a mentoring program for young people who need a greater adult presence in their lives.
- Provide safe-environment training opportunities for all adult leaders, to help them understand the importance of appropriate behavior and boundaries.
- Assign an adult member of the parish as a prayer partner for a young person.
- Team a couple of young people who want to learn a new skill with an adult who has expertise in that area.

Strategy 9: Partnering with Parents and Families

Families and faith communities share the task of promoting healthy growth. Like every other aspect of youth ministry, pastoral care must extend beyond the framework of ministry to and with youth to include their parents and families. Adolescence challenges parents to understand, adjust to, and respond to a variety of new situations, and even crises. Youth ministry must work to establish a partnership with families in that common task. Possible approaches to promoting family involvement include these:

- Incorporate family involvement into current programming.
- Meet young people in their homes, and get to know their families.
- Form a parent advisory group.
- Provide parallel programs for parents and adolescents.
- Create bridging experiences to help young people connect the content of or the skills learned in a youth program with home life.
- Create in-home resources and activities.
- Develop a parent resource center that can become an information clearinghouse and a lending library.
- Provide parent education and support networks. Newsletters, media centers, access to counselors and other community experts, retreats, marriage enrichment, adult education, intergenerational programs, parenting classes, and gathered and nongathered opportunities should be made available to help parents develop the confidence and competence needed to see their children through the teenage years.

TryThis

Check out these articles in *The Catholic Youth Bible* for scriptural connections to promoting family involvement:

- "Ravens and Vultures" (Prov. 30:17)
- "Celebrating Families" (Sir. 3:1–16)
- "The Christian Family" (Col. 3:18—4:1)

Strategy 10: Culturally Relevant Programming

A multicultural approach to positive youth development views ethnicity and culture as core features of identity and behavior. Under such an approach, all youth are made to feel welcome and empowered. All adults are trained to be culturally competent. Program participants and their families are equitably represented on advisory councils, and program content is culturally appropriate and relevant to the needs of the participants.

Youth ministry programming can help young people learn about, understand, and appreciate people with backgrounds different from their own. Even churches that are located in homogeneous communities—communities without a multicultural population—can design programs that convey the value of diversity and that create opportunities for multicultural awareness and appreciation. Such programs can counteract prejudice, racism, and discrimination, and can diminish the harmful consequences of those attitudes. Possible approaches to promoting cultural diversity include these:

- Develop prayer experiences that incorporate stories of saints from various cultures and nations.
- Host an international festival with foods from many nations.
- Invite people from different ethnic groups to speak to the young people about their cultures' histories, people, customs, and so on.
- Attend a Mass given in another language.
- Provide programs in which the young people learn the Church's teaching on issues such as racism and on how to apply the teachings to their lives. See the U.S. bishops' Web site, *www.usccb.org,* for pastoral letters, books, and other resources.

Strategy 11: Community Networking

Churches need to work with other community organizations in a common effort to promote healthy adolescent development. Sharing resources, cosponsoring programs, and mobilizing the community to address youth issues are only some of the ways churches and youth-serving organizations can work together for the common good of all young people. Possible approaches to community involvement include these:

- Develop and distribute a directory of recommended counseling resources that young people and their families can use for assistance in times of trouble.
- Create a calendar that lists recommended parish and community events for youth and families.
- Convene a community forum of leaders of youth-serving organizations. Use the forum to build a comprehensive, communitywide approach to positive youth development.

TryThis

Check out these articles in *The Catholic Youth Bible* for scriptural connections to promoting cultural diversity:
◆ "Korean Festival Customs" (Lev. 23:9–44)
◆ "The Tent and the Circle" (Isa. 40:22–23)
◆ "Jesus Is the Light of Life!" (John 8:12–59)
◆ "Don't Forget the Shoulders You Stand On" (Acts 6:8—7:60)

TryThis

Check out these articles in *The Catholic Youth Bible* for scriptural connections to community involvement:
◆ "Living the Covenant Today!" (Josh. 24:1–28)
◆ "The Principle of *Ujamaa*" (Matt. 16:25)
◆ "A Great Team" (Rom. 12:1–8)

All ministers need to be much more aware of the services offered within the local, diocesan, and state communities, and how to plug adolescents into those services. We need to be consultative and collaborative in working with the groups that influence our young people. Many times we seem to compete for the same resources rather than cooperatively utilize them. We also need to join forces with libraries, hospitals, social-service agencies, and businesses to lobby for change. Young people risk being isolated unless we, as youth ministers, can help foster radical relatedness, relationships and connections with people who may be different from us.

Strategy 12:
Growth and Healing Through Prayer and Sacraments

If the Church is to truly care for its young people, it must first of all be a prayerful community in every aspect. The sacrament of Reconciliation can be a starting point for pastoral care. The power of healing, reconciling, sustaining, and comforting that is available through that sacrament can be profound in the life of a young person. We must also examine the pastoral possibilities that exist when the community celebrates the Eucharist, particularly when young people are involved in planning and ministry roles. The Liturgy of the Hours, the stations of the cross, fasting, parish missions, community service, and retreats can all emphasize the need for ongoing conversion—turning to God as our source, salvation, and sustenance. Possible approaches to using the power of prayer and the sacraments include these:

- Encourage young people to get involved in a liturgical ministry.
- Invite young people to work with the parish liturgist to plan a parishwide prayer or reconciliation service.
- Include young people in key liturgical roles during Holy Week and the Easter Vigil.
- Provide opportunities for young people to be involved with a prayer vigil or perpetual adoration.

Conclusion

As Church, we play a critical role in determining the quality of life of our children and adolescents. Pastoral care does not have to be complicated or extraordinary. It simply means taking advantage of ordinary opportunities to respond to people where they are, on *their* holy ground. We must provide a vision of hope and a perception of opportunity by ministering the way Jesus did, that is, through availability, vulnerability, compassion, integrity, and the refusal to do it alone.

TryThis

Check out these articles in *The Catholic Youth Bible* for scriptural connections to prayer and the sacraments:
- "A Lord's Prayer Reflection" (Matt. 6:5–15)
- "Unanswered Prayer" (Mark 11:24)
- "The Peace Prayer of Saint Francis of Assisi" (Eph. 6:10–17)
- "The Making of a Prayer" (James 5:13)

Recommended Resources

Books for Youth to Read

- Bass, Dorothy C., and Don C. Richter, editors. *Way to Live: Christian Practices for Teens.* Nashville, TN: Upper Room Books, 2002.
- Benson, Peter L., Pamela Espeland, and July Galbraith. *What Teens Need to Succeed: Proven, Practical Ways to Shape Your Own Future.* Minneapolis: Free Spirit Publishing, 1998.
- Covey, Sean. *The Seven Habits of Highly Effective Teens.* New York: Fireside Books, 1998.
- Holtz, Lou, and Matt Smith. *A Teen's Game Plan for Life.* Notre Dame, IN: Sorin Books, 2002.

Books for Parents to Read

- Benson, Peter L., Pamela Espeland, and July Galbraith. *What Kids Need to Succeed: Proven, Practical Ways to Raise Good Kids.* Minneapolis: Free Spirit Publishing, 1998.
- Hopson, Darlene Powell, Derek S. Hopson, and Thomas Clavin. *Raising the Rainbow Generation: Teaching Your Children to Be Successful in a Multicultural Society.* New York: Fireside Books, 1993.
- Pipher, Mary. *The Shelter of Each Other: Rebuilding Our Families.* New York: Putnam Publishing Group, 1996.
- *Raising Faithful Older Adolescents.* Minneapolis: Augsburg Fortress Publishers, 2001.
- Wolf, Anthony E. *Get Out of My Life, but First Could You Drive Me and Cheryl to the Mall: A Parent's Guide to the New Teenager,* revised and updated. New York: Farrar, Straus and Giroux, 2002.

Books for the Parish

- Benson, Peter L. *All Kids Are Our Kids: What Communities Must Do to Raise Caring and Responsible Children and Adolescents.* San Francisco: Jossey-Bass, Publishers, 1997.
- Roehlkepartain, Eugene. *Building Assets in Congregations: A Practical Guide for Helping Youth Grow Up Healthy.* Minneapolis: Search Institute, 1998.
- Rowatt, G. Wade, Jr. *Adolescents in Crisis: A Guidebook for Parents, Teachers, Ministers, and Counselors.* Louisville, KY: Westminster/John Knox Press, 2001.

Web Sites

- **Character Counts!** works to build character by teaching the six pillars of character: trustworthiness, respect, responsibility, fairness, caring, and citizenship. Free teaching tools and other materials are available at its Web site, *www.charactercounts.org.*

- **Girls and Boys Town** is a leader in the treatment and care of abused, abandoned, and neglected girls and boys. It provides training and resources for parents and other adults, as well as a Web site, *www.girlsandboystown.org,* with information for young people. Another service of Girls and Boys Town is a Web site just for parents, *www.parenting.org.*

- **The Search Institute** provides information on forty developmental assets—positive experiences, relationships, opportunities, and personal qualities that young people need in order to grow up healthy, caring, and responsible. See its Web site, *www.search-institute.org.*

- **Way to Live** is an online support resource for adults and teens that is based on the book *Way to Live: Christian Practices for Teens,* edited by Dorothy C. Bass and Don C. Richter. To download a leader's guide, visit the Web site, *www.waytolive.org/waytolive_leaders_guide.pdf.*

15

Retreats and Extended Events

Pastoral Care Themes and Retreats

Retreats have proven to be a powerful strategy for engaging the hearts, minds, and spirits of young people. A retreat is often the catalyst a young person needs to rethink priorities, sort out thoughts, and make adjustments in attitudes or behaviors. It is an opportunity for deep prayer and reflection, a time to become aware again of God's loving care. It is often a time for hearing new ideas and rethinking old ones. And finally, a retreat can be a time to connect with adult role models who are committed to Gospel living and willing to walk part of the journey toward wholeness and holiness with teens. In other words, a retreat can be the ideal vehicle for offering effective pastoral care to young people.

Following are two outlines for combining sessions in this manual into daylong retreats, and one outline for creating an extended session. You could also add Try This activities, Live It options and actions, and community-building activities to create overnight and weekend retreats. Be creative. You will undoubtedly come up with many more ideas for adapting the sessions in this manual to a format that best suits the young people with whom you work.

Note: For assistance in implementing and developing retreats, see *Vine and Branches 1,* by Maryann Hakowski (Winona, MN: Saint Mary's Press, 1992).

Retreat 1: Sexuality and Dating

This retreat outline uses the material in chapter 4, "Dating Relationships," and chapter 12, "Sexuality and Spirituality." It is designed to be a daylong retreat (including breaks). To create a longer retreat, you might also add material from chapter 2, "Faith and Friendship," or chapter 6, "Choices and Decisions."

Suggested Schedule

- Icebreakers and bond-building activities: selected from other resources (30 minutes)
- Focusing (chapter 4): "Guess Test" (10 minutes)
- Discussion (chapter 4): "The Ideal Date" (10 minutes)
- Presentation and Discussion (chapter 4): "Looking for Love" (25 minutes)
- Short break
- Discussion (chapter 4, Live It): "Why do they always . . . ?" (30 minutes)
- Reflection (chapter 4, adaptation of Pray It): "Dating Friends" (20 minutes)
- Brainstorming (chapter 4, Live It): "CREATIVE dating" (20 minutes)
- Discussion (chapter 4): "A Dating Creed" (15 minutes)
- Long break or meal
- Focusing (chapter 12): "Human Beings, Sexual Beings" (15 minutes)
- Presentation and Discussion (chapter 12): "Relating with Integrity" (15 minutes)
- Continuum (chapter 12): "Physical Intimacy Timeline" (20 minutes)
- Creative Activity (chapter 12, Live It): "APPLE prints" (30 minutes)
- Short break
- Discussion and Scriptural Reflection (chapter 12, Live It): "Second chances" (30 minutes)
- Reflection (chapter 12): "I Learned, but I Wonder" (10 minutes)
- Prayer (chapter 12, Pray It): "Holy of Holies" (15 minutes)

Retreat 2: Managing Stress, Facing Change

This retreat outline uses the material in chapter 7, "Managing Life's Ups and Downs," chapter 9, "Dealing with Life's Changes," and chapter 13, "Finding Hope." It is designed to be a daylong retreat (including breaks). To create a longer retreat, you might add material from chapter 11, "Helping Peers in Crisis," at the end of the session. You might also bring in someone to talk about relaxation techniques, time management, meditation, coping skills, and so forth.

Suggested Schedule

- Icebreakers and bond-building activities: selected from other resources (30 minutes)
- Focusing (chapter 7): "Keeping Things Afloat" (15 minutes)
- Discussion (chapter 7): "Stressful Issues" (30 minutes)
- Discussion (chapter 7, Live It): "Fight or flight"; or Scripture Search (chapter 7, Live It): "Scriptural struggles" (15 minutes)
- Reflection (chapter 7): "SOARing Through Life" (15 minutes)

- Short break
- Focusing (chapter 9): "The Category Is . . ." (15 minutes)
- Discussion (chapter 9): "Change and the Continuum of Loss" (20 minutes)
- Reflection (chapter 9): "Changes and Losses in My Life"; combined with an adaptation of Prayer (chapter 9, Pray It): "Losses and Learnings" (25 minutes)
- Discussion (chapter 7, Live It): "Where is God?" (15 minutes)
- Long break or meal
- Discussion (chapter 9, Live It): "Loss in the Scriptures" (60 minutes)
- Discussion (chapter 9): "Loss Lifelines" (20 minutes)
- Short break
- Focusing and Discussion (chapter 13): "True Happiness" (20 minutes)
- Discussion (chapter 13): "Making Connections" (20 minutes)
- Reflection (chapter 13): "Finding HOPE" (20 minutes)
- Art Activity (chapter 9, Live It): "Hope markers" (30 minutes)
- Prayer (chapter 13): "My Greatest Hope" (15 minutes)

Extended Session: Honoring Myself and Others

This outline for an extended session uses the material in chapter 3, "Made in God's Image," and chapter 5, "Accepting and Honoring Others." It is designed to last approximately 4 hours (including breaks). To create a day-long retreat, you might add material from chapter 8, "Handling Anger, Managing Conflict."

Suggested Schedule
- Icebreakers and bond-building activities: selected from other resources (20 minutes)
- Focusing (chapter 3): "Making a List and Checking It Twice" (15 minutes)
- Reflection (chapter 3, adapted from Pray It): "I'd Like the World to Know" (15 minutes)
- Short break
- Small-Group Discussion (chapter 3): "Critiquing the Culture" (20 minutes)
- Group Project (chapter 3, Try This for "Wrap-Up: Sentence Starters"): Rewriting Psalm 139 (30 minutes)
- Short break
- Reflection and Discussion (chapter 5): "Have You Ever . . . ?" (25 minutes)
- Small-Group Discussion (chapter 5): "The Next Time . . ." (15 minutes)
- Prayer (chapter 5, Pray It): "Living as Peacemakers" (15 minutes)

Other Combinations

The following combinations could be used to form extended sessions or daylong retreats:

- *Peer ministry retreat.* chapter 11, "Helping Peers in Crisis," and chapter 13, "Finding Hope"
- *Extended program for parents and teens.* chapter 8, "Handling Anger, Managing Conflict," and chapter 10, "Parent-Teen Communication: An Intergenerational Session"
- *Extended session for high school seniors.* chapter 6, "Choices and Decisions," and chapter 9, "Dealing with Life's Changes"
- *Retreat on personal, relational, and sexual integrity.* chapter 3, "Made in God's Image," chapter 6, "Choices and Decisions," and chapter 12, "Sexuality and Spirituality"
- *Retreat on struggles in relationships.* chapter 2, "Faith and Friendship," selected material from chapter 5, "Accepting and Honoring Others," and chapter 8, "Handling Anger, Managing Conflict"

16 Supporting Young People and Families in Crisis

Some adolescent behavior, irritating or worrisome to parents or leaders, is not dangerous for the teenager. Other behavior, however, if it is intense and persistent, may be a sign of deeper and more severe problems that can have serious consequences for the teenager's well-being. Serious disturbances, evident in only about 20 percent of all adolescents, sometimes have their roots in childhood. However, some disturbances, such as anorexia nervosa, appear for the first time during adolescence.

As a youth ministry leader or catechist, you will probably encounter serious situations in the youth with whom you minister. This chapter provides resources for you to use as you experience disturbing issues and crisis situations with adolescents. In the following sections, you will find resources and guidance to help you provide immediate pastoral care and refer situations to professional counselors:

- "Warning Signs." This section helps you know what to look for and pay attention to in the behavior of the adolescents you encounter.
- "Principles of Caring for Adolescents in Crisis." These principles provide guidance to you by identifying the context for pastoral care. They are divided between awareness principles, which guide your stance, and assessment principles, which broaden the needed understanding for assessing serious situations.
- "Principles for Caring Actions." Sometimes actions that we think should be caring and helpful turn out not to be. These principles help you to understand your role and to be clear with a young person as you seek to help them in a crisis.
- "Crisis Hotline Services." This resource identifies a hotline for you and for youth and their parents to use in crisis situations.
- "Pastoral Care Ideas." This section provides ideas and resources for specific crisis issues:
  - substance abuse
  - eating disorders

○ sexual abuse
○ depression
○ suicidal tendencies
○ divorce

Warning Signs

The following behaviors may be signs of emotional disturbance in adolescents:

- The adolescent is withdrawn for long periods of time and shows no interest in others.
- The adolescent has no friends of the same age and is not integrated into a peer group.
- The adolescent is docile, never acts independently, and never initiates activities.
- The adolescent continually runs away from home or school.
- The adolescent frequently gets into fights, physically abuses others, and shows unrelenting anger over minor irritations.
- The adolescent's emotional state moves from high to low without any intervening state or leveling off.
- The adolescent is consistently depressed, is preoccupied with death, or threatens or attempts suicide.
- The adolescent engages in indiscriminate sexual activity with a number of partners.
- The adolescent is often drunk or under the influence of drugs.
- The adolescent loses a dangerous amount of weight or binges on food, vomits frequently after meals, and alternates bouts of excessive eating and starving, out of excessive concern for appearance.

A young person who exhibits those behaviors will not stop or change as a result of lectures, stricter rules, or punishment. Those behaviors are frequently symptoms of a serious disturbance, and professional help may be necessary.

(This section is adapted from Gayle Williams (Dorman), Dick Geldof, and Bill Scarborough, *Living with 10- to 15-Year-Olds,* p. 167.)

Principles of Caring for Adolescents in Crisis

Awareness Principles

Egalitarian Partnership

Adults need to be aware of the adolescent's concern to be treated as an equal. By offering friendship first, the adult communicates respect for the teenager as a human being.

Commitment to the Relationship

Young people need to feel that adults will stand by them and be on their side regardless of where their relationships with those adults are headed. Specific ways of expressing the "I'll stand by you" attitude with young people involve such things as taking the initiative in negotiating contacts and appointments, maintaining an interest in their other activities, and discussing future events such as graduation with them.

Openness to New Issues Through a Nondefensive Posture

Nondefensive openness to new issues calls for meeting teenagers in their world of language and ideas. It may even call for meeting them outside the church office, in their homes, at a pizza parlor, or in the church parking lot. An attitude of openness in the relationship will let a teenager's mood set the stage for the depth of the conversation, which strengthens the capacity to care during a crisis.

Privacy

Remember that certain information such as physical abuse and sexual abuse cannot be maintained in secrecy but must be reported to legal authorities. Nevertheless, other information needs to be held in the strictest confidence. Though each person must determine ethically what he or she will hold secret and what must be shared with family or other professionals, all adults must convey an attitude of respect for the boundaries of an adolescent's information. All adults need to communicate clearly with adolescents about information that must be shared. It is better to tell a young person ahead of time than to have him or her discover later that a confidence has been violated.

Understanding the Adolescent

Adults must understand teenagers and communicate to the teens that they know not only their general plight but also their specific problems. Teenagers are often more concerned that their point of view be understood than they are worried about getting their way. Many adolescents cry for understanding from the adult world. They feel that adults have forgotten the pain and perhaps never knew the depth of frustration they experience.

Sensitivity to Gender Issues

Adult leaders need to understand that a person of the same sex may be needed to discuss some problems with teenagers who are in crisis. For example, as soon as possible after learning of sexual abuse or rape, a person of the same sex needs to be available to talk with the victim.

Assessment Principles

Avoid Projection

Adult leaders who do not know themselves well or perhaps are unaware of their own spiritual struggles and psychosocial issues run the danger of seeing their own issues projected onto the screen of the adolescent's life drama. Such "personal issue" blindness makes assessing the adolescent's situation impossible.

Develop a High Level of Self-Awareness

Sensitive ministers know how to use their feelings toward a teenager as a guide to understanding how other people will respond to the teen. For example, an adult might begin to feel hostile or angry toward the teenager who is asking for help. As those angry feelings emerge, the adult can ask: What is it about this teenager that prompts the hostility? Could that same dynamic be contributing to the nature of the crisis? Manipulative teenagers might be sabotaging their own systems of help at home, school, or work. When the manipulation appears to the minister as a reason for feelings of hostility, it can be used as a tool for assessment.

Understand the Developmental Stage and Issues of the Teenager

In emergency crises, developmental issues for the teenager form a lens through which the teen sees the emergency event. Knowing the teenager's developmental issue provides vital information in assessing not only the cause and impact of the crisis, but also the probable resolution of the crisis.

Assess Social Factors

In assessing a crisis, the minister needs to sort out contextual issues from personal issues. For example, a young man who has been arrested for shoplifting may have a personal problem or may in complex ways be reflecting the injustice of his own economic plight. Social factors are a major force in adolescent behavior. If a pattern of certain types of crises arises among a given adolescent group, that should be seen as a red flag indicating that some larger social issue may be impacting everyone in the group. Of course, personal peer pressure may actually be accounting for the universality of the crisis. For example, if a disproportionate number of teenagers are dealing with suicidal thoughts within a youth group, it could be that they have formed a suicide pact, or that social pressures are generating a pervasive sense of hopelessness in their society.

Understand the Faith Issues of the Adolescent

Knowing faith-development and spiritual-formation processes enables the adult leader to assess the pilgrimage of the adolescent. Unresolved faith issues may precipitate a crisis. For example, a teenager may become angry at God because a sibling had an accident, and blame God for it. In anger at God, the teenager may begin acting out irresponsibly. Assessing faith issues also involves looking at the stage of moral development. Many youth are doing the right things, but for the wrong reasons. For example, they may be living within the boundaries of acceptable behavior only out of fear of being caught. Those youth have not matured to the point of following the right path for the sake of love of self, God, and others. Faith- and moral-development issues are an important part of assessment because of their impact on youths' decision-making processes. Young people often make decisions concerning their response to a particular crisis without sufficient faith development and mature moral development.

Assess the Family Environment

Effective adult leaders know how to assess the adequacy of a family structure and the health of family relationships. Ministers stand in a unique role for such assessment because often they will have a relationship with the family as well as the youth.

(This section is adapted from Sharon Reed, *Guides to Youth Ministry*, pp. 70–74.)

Principles for Caring Actions

Listen Twice As Much As You Talk

Careful listening avoids interruptions, gives undivided attention, and frequently checks out the accuracy of understanding. The importance of listening to the young person's hidden message as well as the story line of the crisis cannot be overstated. Adolescents frequently do not know the issues underlying their story lines. The hidden message is often beyond their awareness. Don't protect, but do offer insights for their consideration.

Guide the Decision-Making Process

When the crisis event is fresh and emotions are still raw, providing guidance not only lowers anxiety but also increases the probability that another crisis will not be precipitated by unwise action. In guiding teenagers' decision-making, one must be careful not to be a shallow advice giver. Guidance at its best draws out the issues and clarifies the alternatives, but leaves the decision-making as a responsibility for the youth. After decisions have been finalized, the youth may need help to implement them.

Be an Advocate for the Adolescent

Advocating for the adolescent might involve interfacing with agencies or authorities on the youth's behalf. Teenagers may receive little respect when they confront legal, academic, or even economic systems. Supporting them might mean going to court with them, finding someone who can visit with them in the counselor's office at school, or accompanying them to discuss the crisis with their parents. Youth need to feel that you are present with them emotionally even when you are not present physically.

Express and Receive Honest Emotions

Revealing one's emotions permits the young person to ventilate negative, noxious feelings. By sharing one's own emotions, the caregiver models for the adolescent appropriate avenues of emotional release. Providing a safe environment for ventilation reduces the possibility of the teenager acting out dangerously at a later time.

Hold Out Realistic Hope in a Crisis

Hope is grounded in our system of faith. Teens cannot navigate life from a borrowed perspective on faith. Until they own a faith perspective, they remain rather hopeless. This principle of hope should not minimize the reality of danger, but can focus on possibilities for the future. Frequently adolescents look only to the past, which makes them feel hopeless about themselves, their environment, and the future. Those who provide care for adolescents who are in crisis do well to refocus the adolescents' attention on the future with an attitude of hope.

(This section is adapted from Sharon Reed, *Guides to Youth Ministry,* pp. 75–77.)

Crisis Hotline Services

The Girls and Boys Town national hotline number is 800-448-3000. That hotline is a 24-hour crisis, resource, and referral service. Accredited by the American Association of Suicidology, the hotline is staffed by trained counselors who can respond to questions every day of the week, 365 days a year. Its services are available free of charge to every concerned adult and child in all fifty states, the District of Columbia, Puerto Rico, the Virgin Islands, and Canada.

Children and parents, and other concerned adults may call with any serious concern, such as physical and sexual abuse, alcoholism, drug abuse, parenting problems, suicide, running away, and school problems.

Hotline operators are highly trained professionals who have college degrees or experience in human services and counseling. The staff includes Spanish-speaking operators, who are available 24 hours a day. A TDD machine allows counselors to communicate with those who are hearing impaired. (The TDD number is 800-448-1833.)

The hotline has a computer database of fifty thousand local agencies and services around the service area. Operators, therefore, not only counsel callers on the telephone but also can refer them to helpful people and services located in their hometowns. The hotline staff actively follow up to see that contact or placement with local agencies has occurred.

Pastoral Care Ideas

For Youth Struggling with Substance Abuse

- Refer adolescents to an Alateen group in your community. If one does not exist, consider organizing a group in your parish or supporting the formation of Alateen groups alongside the Alcoholics Anonymous groups in the community.
- Organize or support organizations like Students Against Drunk Drivers.
- Work with community and school leaders in developing broad-based chemical-dependency education programs.
- Work with parents to encourage the formation of covenants and pledges of no drinking and driving.
- Deal with depression, anxiety, and the inability to express anger, which frequently contribute to adolescent drug abuse. Focusing on the adolescent's self-identity from a positive point of view will encourage the adolescent to acknowledge the problem of substance abuse and to seek further help.
- Sustaining the adolescent in the ongoing struggle may mean being on call like an Alcoholics Anonymous sponsor if the adolescent is tempted to return to the abuse.
- Facilitate reconciliation between the former substance abuser and her or his family and friends. Reconciliation with peers may mean serving as a bridge to introduce the former substance abuser into a new peer group and then help her or him find a new role and a new place in the Christian community.
- Develop the social skills (life skills) of adolescents through involvement in support groups and by teaching them appropriate behavior.
- Develop a recommended list of counselors and treatment centers. Look for centers that provide at least the following features: a positive, supportive climate; drug-free objectives; attention to life skills; family involvement in treatment; and arrangements for aftercare.

For Youth Struggling with Eating Disorders

- Recognize that because eating disorders indicate low self-esteem, you'll need to reach out. Don't be afraid to demonstrate your concern by asking about it. Take advantage of the "teachable moment" that occurs when you have optimum possibility for honest response and enough time to talk.
- If the young person admits a problem exists, suggest appropriate professional help. If the young person denies that a problem exists, talk with the parents and share your suspicions and concerns.
- Tell the young person that you plan to share your concern with his or her parents or guardians. Invite the young person to be with you when you talk to the adults, so that your behavior is not misinterpreted or considered malicious in any way.
- Support the parents or guardians in attempts to get help, even though you risk the anger of the young person.
- The possibility of involvement in a specialized treatment program does not preclude the teenager's need for continuing involvement with those who are friends. Even after a referral has been successfully made, adult leaders still have pastoral responsibility. Encourage them to share their feelings, and invite them to join with you in seeking God's wisdom and comfort through prayer.

   (This section is adapted from Anthony Campalo, Wayne Rice, and Rich Van Pelt, *Intensive Care*, pp. 165–170.)

For Youth Struggling with Sexual Abuse

Dealing with abused adolescents is a long process that requires care and commitment. The following needs are guiding lights for your ministry with them:

- An abused adolescent needs some help in disclosing that vulnerable secret. A report to a child protection agency is appropriate, useful, and mandated. Obviously, steps need to be taken to ensure that the abuse stops. The police and welfare departments can arrange shelter if the victim is in immediate danger. Many public and private agencies can report, protect, or help the abuse victim. Abuse must be reported to the police or welfare departments; they will contact the parents.
- Once the abuse has been disclosed, the family will be in crisis. Every family member needs care, and the children are easily overlooked. Pay attention; inquire about their feelings and fears; acknowledge them as valuable and important persons.
- The abused young person needs to hear repeatedly one all-important message: "No one deserves to be abused; it's not your fault. You did nothing wrong. I'm glad you have survived [or weren't hurt worse]. You are not alone; abuse happens to many people. Abuse is against the law."

- Be available to the abused adolescent in a consistently caring way. Abused adolescents need someone who can tolerate their low self-esteem and attempts to clarify the love-pain confusion. If you become an important person in the adolescent's life, those mixed messages will be tested on you. Consistency is the key. Maintain a supportive relationship with the young person during the problem-solving process. Because the abused adolescent's world can be chaotic, you need to be a person of your word—responsible, steady, and faithful in your promises.

- Abuse has long-term negative effects; appropriate intervention gives adolescents a chance to find solutions to personal and family problems. Any adolescent who has been sexually assaulted needs professional help. If the abuse was ongoing yet kept secret, the duration of the therapy will be longer than for abuse that is reported after the first offense. Treatment needs to be provided by an objective professional who has been specially trained. The therapy will help the adolescent integrate the abuse into a total life experience and become a survivor.

(This section is adapted from Virginia D. Ratliff and J. Bill Ratliff, "Abused Children.")

For Youth Facing Depression

- In working with depressed adolescents, one needs to give extra attention to the rather nonspecific characteristics of one's relationship with them. Depressed adolescents can be even more difficult and resistant than those with behavior disorders. Warmth, empathy, and congruence are hallmarks of all effective relationships, but are particularly important in dealing with depressed teenagers.

- An aggressive, intense relationship may frighten a depressed adolescent and cause him or her to withdraw even more. Sensitive, supportive caring on a regular but brief basis is better for building the relationship.

- Activity is an important step in overcoming depression. Though many depressed people will want to wait until they feel like participating in something and thus never get around to being involved, adolescents who can force themselves into action find that the depression lessens and new feelings evolve. Basically, they act their way into new feelings, rather than feeling their way into acting differently.

- Music is the language in which many teens address their mood issues. Just as Saul was soothed by David's playing the lyre, many adolescents identify with and find release through music. While certain music addresses their depression, other music suggests new feelings. Body movements, exercise, and dancing can also facilitate mood shifts.

(This section is adapted from G. Wade Rowatt Jr., *Pastoral Care with Adolescents in Crisis,* p. 122.)

For Youth Dealing with Suicidal Tendencies

- Ask direct, straightforward questions in a calm manner. For example, "Are you thinking about hurting yourself?"
- Assess the seriousness of the suicidal intent by asking questions about feelings, important relationships, other people the person has talked with, and the amount of thought given to the means to be employed. If a gun, pills, rope, or other means has been procured and a specific plan has been developed, the situation is very dangerous. Stay with the person until help arrives.
- Listen and be supportive, without giving false reassurances.
- Encourage the young person to get professional help, and help the person do so.
- Do not ignore warning signs.
- Do not refuse to talk about suicide if a young person approaches you.
- Do not react with horror, disapproval, or repulsion.
- Do not offer false reassurances ("Everything will be all right.") or platitudes and simple answers ("You should be thankful for . . .").
- Do not abandon the young person after the crisis has passed or after professional counseling has begun.

(This section is adapted from Gayle Williams (Dorman), Dick Geldof, and Bill Scarborough, *Living with 10- to 15-Year-Olds*, pp. 165–166.)

For Youth Struggling with Divorce

- Teach teens how to move through the grief process most effectively by dealing with feelings in healthy ways. Instead of taking it out on someone or something or holding it in, talk it out. Choosing that healthy and functional option allows teens to express—with assertion, honesty, and openness—what they think, feel, need, and want.
- Teach young people how to negotiate with parents. Negotiation is trying to resolve conflicts through communication and compromise, as opposed to either avoiding confrontation or forcing one's own choice on someone.
- Encourage young people to take responsibility for understanding who they are and letting others know what they need and want.
- Provide young people with the tools to learn how God reaches out and cares for them—even in the toughest times.
- Encourage participation in church life—worship, youth ministry activities, and intergenerational gatherings.

(This section is adapted from Stephen Murray and Randy Smith, *Divorce Recovery for Teenagers*, pp. 52–54.)

Acknowledgments

The scriptural quotations contained herein are from the New Revised Standard Version of the Bible, Catholic Edition (NRSV). Copyright © 1993 and 1989 by the Division of Christian Education of the National Council of the Churches of Christ in the United States of America. All rights reserved.

The material labeled *CFH* or *Catholic Faith Handbook* is from *The Catholic Faith Handbook for Youth,* by Brian Singer-Towns et al. (Winona, MN: Saint Mary's Press, 2004). Copyright © 2004 by Saint Mary's Press. All rights reserved.

The material labeled *CYB* or *Catholic Youth Bible* is from *The Catholic Youth Bible,* first edition (Winona, MN: Saint Mary's Press, 2000). Copyright © 2000 by Saint Mary's Press. All rights reserved.

The information about the goals and vision for ministry with adolescents on pages 9–10 is from *Renewing the Vision: A Framework for Catholic Youth Ministry,* by the United States Conference of Catholic Bishops' (USCCB) Department of Education (Washington, DC: USCCB, 1997), pages 1–2. Copyright © 1997 by the USCCB, Inc. All rights reserved.

The Pray It activity on pages 30–32 is adapted from *Growing in Wisdom, Age, and Grace,* by Thomas Zanzig with Marilyn Kielbasa (Winona, MN: Saint Mary's Press, 1996), pages 60–61. Copyright © 1996 by Saint Mary's Press. All rights reserved.

The activities "Guess Test" on pages 43–44, "The Ideal Date" on page 44 and "Looking for Love" on pages 44–46 are adapted from *Dating and Love,* by Michael Theisen (Winona, MN: Saint Mary's Press, 1996), pages 20, 20–21, and 22–23, respectively. Copyright © 1996 by Saint Mary's Press. All rights reserved.

The activity "Needs and Obstacles" on pages 55–56 is adapted from *Finding Your Personal Style,* by Marilyn Kielbasa (Winona, MN: Saint Mary's Press, 1996), pages 52–53. Copyright © 1996 by Saint Mary's Press. All rights reserved.

The Pray It activity on pages 57–58, the prayer on resource 2, and the session "Anger, Conflict, and PEACE," on pages 82–85, are adapted from *Becoming a Peacemaker,* by Gail Daniels Hassett (Winona, MN: Saint Mary's Press, 1996), pages 24–25, 24–25, and 29–37, respectively. Copyright © 1996 by Saint Mary's Press. All rights reserved.

The activity "LISTENing for a Solution" on pages 64–65 is adapted from *Growing in Christian Morality,* by Julia Ahlers, Barbara Allaire, and Carl Koch (Winona, MN: Saint Mary's Press, 1996), pages 78–82. Copyright © 1996 by Saint Mary's Press. All rights reserved.

The activity "A Piece of the Puzzle" on pages 65–66 is adapted from *Prayer Works for Teens Book 4,* by Lisa-Marie Calderone-Stewart (Winona, MN: Saint Mary's Press, 1997), pages 32–34. Copyright © 1997 by Saint Mary's Press. All rights reserved.

The definition of discernment on page 68 is from the *HarperCollins Encyclopedia of Catholicism,* edited by Richard P. McBrien (San Francisco: HarperSanFrancisco, 1995), page 419. Copyright © 1995 by HarperCollins Publishers.

The activities "Stressful Issues" on pages 73–74 and "SOARing Through Life" on pages 74–75, and handouts 5 and 6 are adapted from, and resource 4CD is from *Taking Charge: Managing Life's Struggles,* by Marilyn Kielbasa and Michael Theisen (Winona, MN: Saint Mary's Press, 1996), pages 31–35, 49–50, 42, 64, and 37–38, respectively. Copyright © 1996 by Saint Mary's Press. All rights reserved.

The quote from Heraclitus on page 93 and on handout 11 is taken from John Bartlett's *Familiar Quotations,* sixteenth edition, edited by Justin Kaplan (Boston: Little, Brown and Company, 1992), page 62. Copyright © 1992 by Little, Brown and Company.

The "still wondering" option on page 99 is adapted from *Death, Grief, and Christian Hope,* by Nancy Marrocco (Winona, MN: Saint Mary's Press, 1997), page 24. Copyright © 1997 by Saint Mary's Press. All rights reserved.

The excerpted list on page 109 is adapted from *People Skills: How to Assert Yourself, Listen to Others, and Resolve Conflicts,* by Robert Bolton, PhD (New York: Simon and Schuster, Touchstone Books, 1986), pp. 15–16. Copyright © 1979 by Simon and Schuster.

The activity on pages 110–111 is adapted from *YouthWorks* (Naugatuck, CT: Center for Ministry Development, 1994), page 5. Copyright © 1994 by the Center for Ministry Development.

The prayer on handout 12 is adapted from *Parent-Teen Relationships,* by Gail Daniels Hassett (Winona, MN: Saint Mary's Press, 1996), page 42. Copyright © 1996 by Saint Mary's Press. All rights reserved.

The activity "Burdens in a Bundle" on pages 119–120 and resource 6 are adapted from *Prayer: Celebrating and Reflecting with Girls,* by Marilyn Kielbasa (Winona, MN: Saint Mary's Press, 2002), pages 62–64 and 65. Copyright © 2002 by Saint Mary's Press. All rights reserved.

The Try This activity about red, yellow, and green zones on pages 128–129 and the activity "Holy of Holies" on pages 130–131 are adapted from, and resource 7 is from *Seeking: Doing Theology with Girls,* by Janet Claussen with Julia Ann Keller (Winona, MN: Saint Mary's Press, 2003), pages 117, 118–119, and 129, respectively. Copyright © 2003 by Saint Mary's Press. All rights reserved.

The quotation on page 134 is from the English translation of the *Catechism of the Catholic Church* for use in the United States of America, page 882. Copyright © 1994 by the United States Catholic Conference, Inc.—Libreria Editrice Vaticana.

The activity "True Happiness" on pages 135–136 is adapted from *Scripture Walk Senior High Discipleship: Bible-Based Sessions for Teens,* by Nora Bradbury-Haehl (Winona, MN: Saint Mary's Press, 2000), pages 43–44. Copyright © 2000 by Saint Mary's Press. All rights reserved.

The warning signs on page 160 and the ideas for youth dealing with suicidal tendencies on page 168 are adapted from *Living with 10- to 15-Year-Olds: A Parent Education Curriculum,* by Gayle Williams (Dorman), Dick Geldof, and Bill Scarborough (Carrboro, NC: Center for Early Adolescence, 1982), pages 167 and 165–166. Copyright © 1982 by the Center for Early Adolescence, University of North Carolina at Chapel Hill. Used with permission of Gayle Williams (Dorman).

The principles of caring for adolescents in crisis on pages 161–163 and the principles for caring actions on pages 165–166 are adapted from *Guides to Youth Ministry: Pastoral Care,* edited by Sharon Reed (New Rochelle, NY: Don Bosco Multimedia, 1993), pages 70–74 and 75–77. Copyright © 1993 by Don Bosco Multimedia. Used with permission of the Center for Ministry Development.

The ideas for youth struggling with eating disorders on pages 166 are adapted from *Intensive Care: Helping Teenagers in Crisis,* by Anthony Campalo, Wayne Rice, and Rich Van Pelt (Grand Rapids, MI: Zondervan Publishing, Youth Specialties, 1988), pages 165–170. Copyright © 1988 by Youth Specialties, Inc. Used with permission of the Zondervan Corporation.

The ideas for youth struggling with sexual abuse on pages 166–167 are adapted from "Abused Children," by Virginia D. Ratliff and J. Bill Ratliff, in *When Children Suffer: A Sourcebook for Ministry with Children in Crisis,* edited by Andrew D. Lester (Philadelphia: Westminster Press, 1987), page 132. Copyright © 1987 by Andrew D. Lester. Used with permission of Westminster John Knox Press.